HAL

LEARNING DISABILITY
and the social context of caring

Target completion date

Tutor for this topic

Contact number

USING THIS WORKBOOK

The workbook is divided into 'Sessions', covering specific subjects.

In the introduction to each learning pack there is a learner profile to help you assess your current knowledge of the subjects covered in each session.

Each session has clear learning objectives. They indicate what you will be able to achieve or learn by completing that session.

Each session has a summary to remind you of the key points of the subjects covered.

Each session contains text, diagrams and learning activities that relate to the stated objectives.

It is important to complete each activity, making your own notes and writing in answers in the space provided. **Remember this is your own workbook—you are allowed to write on it**.

Now try an example activity.

ACTIVITY

This activity shows you what happens when cells work without oxygen. This really is a physical activity, so please only try it if you are fully fit.

First, raise one arm straight up in the air above your head, and let the other hand rest by your side. Clench both fists tightly, and then open out your fingers wide. Repeat this at the rate of once or twice a second. Try to keep clenching both fists at the same rate. Keep going for about five minutes, and record what you observe.

Stop and rest for a minute. Then try again, with the opposite arm raised this time. Again, record your observations.

Suggested timings are given for each activity. These are only a guide. You may like to note how long it took you to complete this activity, as it may help in planning the time needed for working through the sessions.

Time taken on activity

Time management is important. While we recognise that people learn at different speeds, this pack is designed to take 20 study hours (your tutor will also advise you). You should allocate time during each week for study.

Take some time now to identify likely periods that you can set aside for study during the week.

	Mon	Tues	Wed	Thurs	Fri	Sat	Sun
am							
pm							
eve							

At the end of the learning pack, there is a learning review to help you assess whether you have achieved the learning objectives.

LEARNING DISABILITY
and the social context of caring

Mary Birchenall MA BA RNT RNMH
Course Leader, BHSc modular framework,
School of Health Care Studies, University of Leeds

Susan Baldwin MSc Dip Nursing Studies Cert Ed RNMH
Nursing Lecturer (Learning Disabilities),
School of Health Care Studies, University of Leeds

Jill Morris MA Dip CMMH Cert Ed RNMH
Nursing Lecturer (Learning Disabilities)
School of Health Care Studies, University of Leeds

THE OPEN LEARNING FOUNDATION

CHURCHILL LIVINGSTONE

NEW YORK EDINBURGH LONDON MADRID MELBOURNE SAN FRANCISCO AND TOKYO 1997

CHURCHILL LIVINGSTONE
Medical Division of Longman Group UK Limited

Distributed in the United States of America by Churchill
Livingstone Inc., 650 Avenue of the Americas, New York,
N.Y. 10011, and by associated companies, branches and
representatives throughout the world.

First published 1997

ISBN 0 443 05735 4

British Library of Cataloguing in Publication Data
A catalogue record for this book is available from the
British Library.

Library of Congress Cataloging in Publication Data
A catalog record for this book is available from the
Library of Congress.

Produced through Longman Malaysia, PP

For The Open Learning Foundation

Director of Programmes: Leslie Mapp
Series Editor: Peter Birchenall
Programmes Manager: Kathleen Farren
Production Manager: Steve Moulds

For Churchill Livingstone

Director (Nursing and Allied Health): Peter Shepherd
Project Manager: Valerie Burgess
Project Controller: Derek Robertson
Design Direction: Judith Wright
Sales Promotion Executive: Maria O'Connor

CONTENTS

OPEN LEARNING FOUNDATION
TEAM MEMBERS

Writers: Mary Birchenall
Course Leader, BHSc Modular Framework
School of Health Care Studies, University of Leeds

Susan Baldwin
Nursing Lecturer (Learning Disabilities)
School of Health Care Studies, University of Leeds

Jill Morris
Nursing Lecturer (Learning Disabilities)
School of Health Care Studies, University of Leeds

Editor: Penny Mares

Reviewers: Andrew Lovall
Nurse Tutor,
School of Nursing and Midwifery
University College, Chester

Susan Willis
Nurse Tutor
School of Nursing and Midwifery
University College, Chester

Theresa Adshe
School of Nursing and Midwifery
University College, Chester

Series Editor: Peter Birchenall
OLF Programme Head
Health and Nursing
University of Humberside

THE OPEN LEARNING FOUNDATION

Higher education has grown considerably in recent years. As well as catering for more students, universities are facing the challenge of providing for an increasingly diverse student population. Students have a wider range of backgrounds and previous educational qualifications. There are greater numbers of mature students. There is a greater need for part-time courses and continuing education and professional development programmes.

The Open Learning Foundation helps over 20 member institutions meet this growing and diverse demand – through the production of high-quality teaching and learning materials, within a strategy of creating a framework for more flexible learning. It offers member institutions the capability to increase their range of teaching options and to cover subjects in greater breadth and depth.

It does not enrol its own students. Rather, The Open Learning Foundation, by developing and promoting the greater use of open and distance learning, enables universities and others in higher education to make study more accessible and cost-effective for individual students and for business through offering more choice and more flexible courses.

Formed in 1990, the Foundation's policy objectives are to:

- improve the quality of higher education and training

- increase the quantity of higher education and training

- raise the efficiency of higher education and training delivery.

In working to meet these objectives, The Open Learning Foundation develops new teaching and learning materials, encourages and facilitates more and better staff development, and promotes greater responsiveness to change within higher education institutions. The Foundation works in partnership with its members and other higher education bodies to develop new approaches to teaching and learning.

In developing new teaching and learning materials, the Foundation has:

- a track record of offering customers a swift and flexible response

- a national network of members able to provide local support and guidance

- the ability to draw on significant national expertise in producing and delivering open learning

- complete freedom to seek out the best writers, materials and resources to secure development.

Other titles in this series

INTRODUCTION

This unit provides an introduction to some of the key areas of knowledge about caring for people with a learning disability. Topic areas have been carefully selected to enable the reader to appreciate the breadth of theory that informs this area of care. The unit has been written for carers from a wide range of backgrounds, such as student nurses in the early stages of Branch, experienced healthcare assistants in small group homes and residential social workers. It may also be useful to relatives who are carers.

The unit is presented in six sessions. The first three provide a theoretical background to services for people with a learning disability.

Session One reviews some common causes and associated conditions of learning disability before going on to consider the impact of disability on the individual and the family and the stigma associated with it.

Session Two starts with a historical review of services for people with a learning disability and then moves on to consider the ways in which that history influences present day care.

Session Three explores the meaning of the concept of normalisation and the way it is applied to services.

Sessions Four, Five and Six consider a range of skill developments necessary for the person involved in this field of care.

Session Four introduces some of the basic principles of teaching and helps you to realise your own strengths and limitations in this area.

Session Five, on sexuality, helps you to examine an area of care for people with a learning disability that has been overlooked in the past. Some challenges have been built into this session.

Session Six explores and clarifies the nature of challenging behaviour. Because the challenges made to care services and carers require you to reflect on the way that services have developed and attitudes have modified, this final session represents, in many ways, a synthesis of issues covered in the earlier sessions.

LEARNING PROFILE

This unit explores the social context of caring for people with a learning disability. To identify your own learning needs, you will find it useful to complete the self-assessment questionnaire below. This exercise will help you work out where your needs are greatest and enable you to develop a learning plan to suit your needs.

Work through the learning objectives for each session in the unit, and give yourself a personal score for each objective by ticking the appropriate box.

	Not at all	Partly	Quite well	Very well

Session One

I can:

	Not at all	Partly	Quite well	Very well
● review some common causes of learning disability and significant associated conditions including epilepsy and cerebral palsy	☐	☐	☐	☐
● analyse the social impact of learning disability on the family	☐	☐	☐	☐
● discuss the significance of sibling rivalry in relation to learning	☐	☐	☐	☐
● disability	☐	☐	☐	☐
● analyse the language of disability	☐	☐	☐	☐
● discuss the impact of disability on the individual's life chances.	☐	☐	☐	☐

Session Two

I can:

	Not at all	Partly	Quite well	Very well
● review the history of care of people with learning disabilities	☐	☐	☐	☐
● relate this to the prevailing attitudes of the time	☐	☐	☐	☐
● describe the impact of institutionalisation on individual development	☐	☐	☐	☐
● explain the current structure of care provision	☐	☐	☐	☐
● explain the significance of the mixed economy of care.	☐	☐	☐	☐

Session Three

I can:

	Not at all	Partly	Quite well	Very well
● define what is meant by the term 'normalisation'	☐	☐	☐	☐
● explain the origin of the concept and its early implications for institutional care	☐	☐	☐	☐

	Not at all	Partly	Quite well	Very well

Session Three *continued*

- evaluate normalisation as a principle for practice, and discuss its role in the move to community care for learning disability

| | ☐ | ☐ | ☐ | ☐ |

- identify the impact of unconscious prejudice on the development of human services

| | ☐ | ☐ | ☐ | ☐ |

- explain the concept of a conservative corollary to the principle of normalisation and its importance

| | ☐ | ☐ | ☐ | ☐ |

- identify key accomplishments that services should try to achieve on behalf of users and apply this to an individual case study

| | ☐ | ☐ | ☐ | ☐ |

- review the process of audit for the care environment in relation to the quality of care and the promotion of a 'normal' lifestyle.

| | ☐ | ☐ | ☐ | ☐ |

Session Four

I can:

- evaluate the processes of teaching and learning

| | ☐ | ☐ | ☐ | ☐ |

- plan, implement and evaluate a teaching session

| | ☐ | ☐ | ☐ | ☐ |

- develop a teaching programme for clients in a chosen area of interest

| | ☐ | ☐ | ☐ | ☐ |

- understand and use structured teaching strategies in creating a learning opportunity

| | ☐ | ☐ | ☐ | ☐ |

- develop skills in creating learning programmes for people with limited literacy skills

| | ☐ | ☐ | ☐ | ☐ |

- assist informal carers in developing their own teaching skills.

| | ☐ | ☐ | ☐ | ☐ |

Session Five

I can:

- discuss the development and expression of sexuality

| | ☐ | ☐ | ☐ | ☐ |

- evaluate the impact of learning disability on the development and expression of sexuality

| | ☐ | ☐ | ☐ | ☐ |

- identify some common social attitudes towards the sexuality of people with a learning disability

| | ☐ | ☐ | ☐ | ☐ |

	Not at all	Partly	Quite well	Very well

Session Five *continued*

- analyse the important areas of carer support with respect to sexuality in people with a learning disability ☐ ☐ ☐ ☐
- discuss the legal rights of the person with learning disability, with particular reference to fertility, marriage and pregnancy. ☐ ☐ ☐ ☐

Session Six

I can:

- define challenging behaviour and discuss its characteristics ☐ ☐ ☐ ☐
- describe a range of possible causes of challenging behaviour in people with a learning disability ☐ ☐ ☐ ☐
- consider the integrated functioning of the individual in terms of a theoretical framework of their physical, intellectual, social, emotional and spiritual dimensions ☐ ☐ ☐ ☐
- discuss the social implications of challenging behaviour upon the person with a learning disability ☐ ☐ ☐ ☐
- describe and discuss a behaviourist, therapeutic approach to challenging behaviour, using the behavioural analysis (ABC) chart. ☐ ☐ ☐ ☐

SESSION ONE

The social dimension of learning disability

Introduction

Although the focus of this unit is on the social context of learning disability, some understanding of the causes and of associated conditions is often sought by those who have a caring role. We therefore begin the session with a brief overview of some common causes and conditions, before going on to discuss the impact of learning disability from several different perspectives. We introduce some key concepts and common prejudices about people with a learning disability and discuss the power of language in determining social worth.

Session objectives

When you have completed this session you should be able to:

- review some significant associated conditions including epilepsy and cerebral palsy

- analyse the impact of learning disability upon the family

- discuss the concept of sibling rivalry in relation to learning disability

- analyse the language of disability

- discuss the impact of disability upon the individual's life chances.

1: Causes of learning disabilities and associated conditions

When we examine the causes of learning disability we usually do so from a point of four time periods. These are:

conceptual: genetic and chromosomal defects that can give rise to learning disabilities

pre-natal: from conception to birth of the child

birth: conditions arising as a complication of birth

post-natal: the period after birth.

ACTIVITY I   ALLOW **15** MINUTES

Think about conditions related to learning disability that you have either seen or heard about from colleagues. In the table below list each condition under the heading that you think is most appropriate.

Conceptual	Pre-natal	Birth	Post-natal

Commentary

I imagine you found this activity quite challenging. Let us try to fill in a few gaps. Below you will find a completed table (*Table 1*) to compare with your own (the lists are by no means exhaustive).

Conceptual	Pre-natal	Birth	Post-natal
Chromosomal	drugs	anoxia	drugs
Down's syndrome	smoking	hypoxia	allergies (aspirin)
Klinefelter's syndrome	alcohol	accidental injury	poisons (lead)
	poisons		infections
Turner's syndrome	infections	non-accidental injury	social deprivation
Cri-du-chat syndrome	accidental injury	prematurity	emotional deprivation
Genetic:	pre-eclampsia	prolonged labour	accidental injury
Phenylketonuria	radiation exposure	too much oxygen	
Batten's disease	food poisoning		
		infections	

Table 1: Conditions related to learning disability

2: Associated conditions

Foetal alcohol syndrome

Concerns about the potential ill-effects of alcohol on offspring date back to Greek and Roman mythology. Jones (1973) notes that, 'In Carthage the bridal couple was forbidden wine on their wedding night in order that defective children might not be conceived'. One can only speculate as to how the Carthaginians arrived at this rule, but we must at the same time applaud their partial good sense when we consider the devastating effects alcohol can have on the developing foetus.

The characteristic anomalies of this syndrome are wide ranging. The most common are: facial anomalies, microcephaly, heart and respiratory complications, sleeping difficulties, hyperactivity and behavioural problems.

The varying degrees of intellectual impairment are directly related to the amount of alcohol consumed during the pre-natal phase. Children of mothers who drink heavily during pregnancy are at risk of developing the severest form of foetal alcohol syndrome. A less severe form of the condition is called foetal alcohol effect. This is reported by Little (1990) to have an increased frequency in children born to women who drink moderately or 'socially'. In terms of consumption this would be two or three beers or glasses of wine per day. Although this condition is considered to be a lesser form of foetal alcohol syndrome, it produces the same type of symptoms.

Abel et al. (1987) identified foetal alcohol syndrome as the leading cause of learning disabilities in the western world. Taking evidence from both prospective and retrospective studies, he identified the incidence as 1:9 cases per 1,000 live births. Down's syndrome is placed second on the list with an incidence of 1:6 cases per 1,000 live births.

It must be stressed that these figures are based on diagnosed cases of foetal alcohol syndrome, and do not include the estimated incidence of foetal alcohol effect. Abel suggests that problems related to the diagnosis of the condition may give a false impression of its true extent.

ACTIVITY 2   ALLOW **10** MINUTES

What problems do you think may arise once a child is diagnosed as having foetal alcohol syndrome?

Commentary

I will comment by referring to an article by Abel et al. (1987). You will find that it raises a number of issues which are important to the future care of people with foetal alcohol syndrome, and the lesser known foetal alcohol effect.

Abel suggests that the impact of this diagnosis is twofold. First, a diagnosis of foetal alcohol syndrome may clearly affect the psychological well-being of the child. The medical profession may be wary of placing on a child a diagnosis which has profound anti-social connotations. The diagnosis may affect the development of the child's self-concept, or cause other psychological problems. It may also raise the question of blame, which may in turn affect the mother–child relationship. (Think carefully about this concept for a moment, and ask yourself, would you apportion blame?)

Second, economic factors may affect the social response to this condition. Foetal alcohol syndrome is avoidable. Abel discusses its financial cost to the state and raises the question of who is responsible for shouldering these costs. There is a growing debate about the kinds of treatment that should be available on the National Health Service. For example, some would question whether a heavy cigarette smoker should be eligible for heart by-pass surgery.

Alzheimer's disease

People affected by Down's syndrome face many physical and psychological problems. Possibly the most devastating associated condition is Alzheimer's disease. The gene which causes Alzheimer's disease in later life is situated on the 21st pair of chromosomes, of which a person with Down's syndrome has three.

Alzheimer's disease is a condition marked by changes in the structure and chemical functioning of the brain. It usually has two forms:

1 senile dementia of the Alzheimer type

2 pre-senile dementia of the Alzheimer type.

Senile dementia of the Alzheimer type is by far the most common. Pre-senile dementia is rare, only affecting people younger than 45. However, the second form is the type which affects people with Down's syndrome. As early as 1974, Ellis et al. stated that 'In Down's syndrome the reward for survival beyond the age of 40 is pre-senile dementia'.

Prosser (1989) identified the onset of Alzheimer changes in the structure and chemical composition of the brain in people with Down's syndrome. Yet he identified that these changes were not necessarily accompanied by any clinical indications of dementia.

ACTIVITY 3　　　　　ALLOW 10 MINUTES

Why do you think that clinical indications of Alzheimer's disease are not noticeable in people with Down's syndrome? What factors could explain this?

Commentary

People with Down's syndrome already have impaired cognitive functioning, particularly memory and learning difficulties, and may already exhibit anti-social behaviours, all of which are indicative of Alzheimer's disease. Slight deterioration in their skill level may go unnoticed, and be viewed by the professional carer simply as part of their learning disabilities.

Various assessment formats have been and are being developed to assess the onset of Alzheimer's disease in people with Down's syndrome. For further reading on this subject, I suggest an article by Thompson (1994) who uses a battery of assessment tools.

Cerebral palsy

Cerebral palsy is an umbrella term used to describe a variety of disorders that affect an individual's movement and posture. It arises as a consequence of damage to nerve cells within the areas of the brain that regulate motor activity (actions or doing things). It can occur as a result of anoxia.

Because the damage may occur in any of the motor areas of the brain, differing systems may be present in people affected by this condition.

ACTIVITY 4   ALLOW **15** MINUTES

Have you worked with anyone who had a diagnosis of cerebral palsy? List below the patterns of movements you observed in individuals that you have worked with. When you have compiled your list, try to organise these patterns into three categories.

Commentary

It is likely that you have noted variations on the following three themes: rigidity; flaccid movements; and uncontrolled spasms. These are described by Shanley and Starr (1993) under the headings of spasticity, athetosis and ataxia.

Spasticity is characterised by rigidity of the limbs. You may have seen the difficulties that some clients have in extending and bending their limbs when dressing. It is the most common symptom of cerebral palsy. The cause of this symptom is damage to the cerebral motor cortex.

Athetosis is characterised by involuntary movement of the body. For example, you may have noted the difficulties that some clients have in targeting into and picking up an object, almost as though they were too nervous to complete the task.

The more excited or frustrated the individual becomes the more exaggerated the movements become. The originating cause of this movement is the damage to the basal ganglia.

Ataxia is characterised by poor body balance, unsteady gait and poor hand–eye coordination. Generally, people who suffer from this condition appear 'floppy': the technical term is **hypotonia**. The person would be described as hypotonic. This is caused by damage to the cerebellum.

These three definitions seem clear cut, but the reality is that they are not experienced separately. One individual can have more than one of these conditions, but in varying severity. For example, if the most severe injury is to the cerebral motor cortex the dominant image is of rigidity. There can, however, be additional damage to the basal ganglia, causing jerky movements.

For a more in-depth description of cerebral palsy I refer you to Shanley and Starr (1993).

Epilepsy

Markham (1986) describes epilepsy as 'a symptom of disturbed cerebral function. It consists of episodes in which there is a disturbance of movement, sensation, behaviour or consciousness, caused by an abnormal electrical discharge. The discharge may be confined to that group of cells (focus) or it may spread to the surrounding cells, or to the entire brain.'

Epilepsy is a complex condition which has various manifestations depending on which part of the brain is affected. These different manifestations aid the diagnosis of the condition under two main headings.

1 Those which involve the whole brain, or generalised seizures. There is a loss of consciousness, however brief.

2 Those affecting only part of the brain, or partial seizures. Consciousness is not lost, but may be affected.

ACTIVITY 5   ALLOW 15 MINUTES

What types of symptoms have you observed in clients with epilepsy that led you to believe they were having a seizure?

Did you know what type of seizure it was at the time?

Why do you think it is important to know what kind of seizure the person was having?

Commentary

Figure 1 below describes the symptoms of different types of seizure, and you may be able to match these with the symptoms you have observed in clients. It is important to be able to identify the type of seizure because the treatments are different for each. Comprehensive records must be maintained about the type of seizure, the duration (together with a recording of the person's vital signs), any precipitating factors, the individual's recovery period, and behaviour patterns. One of the symptoms you might have identified, for example, was that someone became very irritable just before losing consciousness. This would be an indication that the person was about to have a seizure. Awareness of this would give the care team time to prepare a safe environment, for example, by sitting the client down.

This kind of detailed information helps build up a picture of the frequency and severity of the seizures. This enables corrections to be made to the client's medicine regime and gives care staff an indication of the type of activities that would be suitable for the individual, whilst at the same time ensuring quality of life and providing opportunities for development.

Type of seizure	Symptoms
Tonic clonic	Intense stiffening of muscles (tonic stage) which progresses to twitching/ jerking of muscles (clonic phase). Person loses consciousness.
Tonic	Intense stiffening of muscles. Loss of consciousness. If the individual is standing they will fall to the ground.
Atonic	Loss of muscle tone. The person flops to the floor.
Myoclonic jerks	Involuntary jerking of muscles. Loss of consciousness.
Absence	A brief lapse of consciousness without warning. No body movements. The person gives the impression of staring into space.
Partial (Focal)	
Simple partial	Disturbances of the senses, e.g. taste and smell sensations. Consciousness remains.
Complex partial	Repetitive and bizarre behaviours, confusion, agitation with impaired or loss of consciousness.

Figure 1: Symptoms of different types of epileptic seizure

Certain factors in our environment can trigger the onset of an epileptic seizure. These include strobe lighting, excessive alcohol consumption, lack of sleep, drugs, and for women, menstruation, possibly due to the changes in hormone levels.

That concludes our brief review of common causes and associated conditions of learning disability. We now move on to consider its impact upon the family.

3: The impact of learning disability upon the family

Disability can of course occur at any point in the family life cycle, but we begin by considering the family whose baby is born with a disabling condition.

ACTIVITY 6	ALLOW 15 MINUTES

Read *Resource 1* in the *Resources Section*, an extract from Charles Hannam's book *Parents and Mentally Handicapped Children*. List some of the reactions experienced by the author at the birth of his son.

Commentary

Some of the reactions Hannam describes are:

- shock

- a desperate need for information

- many questions, particularly about the possibility of a cure

- increased activity

- feelings of disaster

- feelings of guilt

- moving towards breaking point

- a need to kill the child

- fear of the future and of these powerful emotions.

The process of coming to terms with the birth of a disabled child is often referred to as part of a cycle or a life process that moves from shock through to resolution. You may be familiar with this cycle from literature on the grieving process. It is not unrealistic to make links with the grieving process at the birth of a disabled baby, since many parents experience complex feelings of loss, for the able child they had expected, for a past life now radically changed, for 'normal' parenthood, for example.

ACTIVITY 7   ALLOW 5 MINUTES

Try to map out a life cycle showing the stages of movement from shock to resolution that may be part of a family's long-term adjustment after the birth of their disabled baby.

Commentary

Your life cycle should include the following stages, although your wording may differ from mine.

The birth of the baby

Something wrong is identified

Shock is experienced

Numbness, or manic activity occurs

Denial, negotiation, the search for a cure

Grief, helplessness, anger

Passive acceptance as the baby's needs are met

A seeking for information to help understanding

Options for the future are considered

The family begins to develop as a unit

Family solidarity emerges.

Not all families progress through these stages and not all move at the same pace. A family can become stuck in the phase of denial, or only reach a point of resolution or closure after decades of coming to terms with their own feelings of tragedy and loss.

ACTIVITY 8   ALLOW 5 MINUTES

Try to put yourself in Charles Hannam's shoes at the moment he considers killing his son. How do you feel about your decision? What feelings might you have when you realise that you have actually considered this?

Commentary

I suspect that you found this activity rather uncomfortable, for the same reasons that Hannam himself was distressed when he realised what he had thought. You will have to read more of the book on your own to find out why he thought like this. Any parent is likely to feel horrified when they realise that they have considered killing their child and their feelings of guilt may remain for a very long time.

The fact that both parents think similar thoughts may be made worse by their inability to confide in each other. They may feel too embarrassed and concerned for their partner to impose the additional burden of sharing these thoughts. Such a situation can mean that they do not have recourse to their usual patterns of mutual support.

Charles Hannam wrote his story in 1975. In the 1990s parents still express feelings of fear, helplessness and lack of support. Today, however, the emergence of parent support groups, often managed by parents themselves, provides the possibility of sharing experiences and talking through some of the more frightening thoughts and feelings. As a carer in the field of learning disabilities for the past 25 years, I still find it difficult when I meet parents, with children in their late teens or early adulthood, who have never had the opportunity to sit down and discuss their needs and feelings with anyone. Thoughts such as 'it would have been better if he/she had died' remain unspoken, locked in by guilt, causing further and needless pain.

So far we have focused on the family from the perspective of the parents. We now move on to discuss the relationships between brothers and sisters when a disabled child becomes a member of the family.

Siblings

Siblings experience any disruption of family life to the same extent as the parents. This issue has only been recognised relatively recently, as a result of developments in our understanding of childhood; but there has been no lack of evidence that brothers and sisters feel the impact of disability on the family.

ACTIVITY 9   ALLOW 15 MINUTES

Read the extracts in *Resource 2* in the *Resources Section*. How would you expect siblings to react to a disabled brother or sister?

Do these accounts in the extract tally with your expectations? List the various reactions highlighted in the extracts.

Commentary

There are as many ways of reacting to a brother or sister with a learning disability as there are people. The ways in which siblings experience and react to a brother or sister with a disability tend to differ according to age at the birth of the baby and the position in the family of the disabled sibling.

Sibling reactions can include feelings of:

- protection
- jealousy
- love
- fear
- embarrassment
- pleasure.

Your list of reactions highlighted in the extract may have included acceptance, fondness, tolerance, forgiveness, caring, protectiveness and frustration.

Family members share the social stigma of learning disability. We will now go on to explore what this stigma consists of in depth.

4: Stigma and condition visibility

'Condition visibility' refers to the extent that a given condition is easy to see. Linked to this idea is the sociological concept of 'stigma'. The term stigma refers to the process through which a devalued personal characteristic is given a social weight that can redefine the worth of a person. A simple example is found in the phrase, 'once a thief, always a thief'. The stigma is that of 'thief': theft is not valued in our society. Once an individual is labelled a thief, other people assume that any good qualities displayed are overshadowed by the need to steal. So someone who is labelled a thief is unlikely to be trusted, or even believed, because of the assumption that they are dishonest. However, a thief is unlikely to be immediately recognisable in every-day life; it is only in the world of cartoons that burglars wear a mask and carry a bag labelled 'LOOT'. The condition of 'thief' may carry a stigma, but it is not a condition that is visible and stigmatised in the way that old age, disability and skin colour often are.

Let us now consider the idea of stigma and condition visibility in relation to learning disability. As a culture we value many visible aspects of the human body, in particular:

Condition visibility: *A disability or disfigurement that is noticeable to the casual observer.*

Stigma: *A negative value attributed to a mental, emotional or physical condition.*

- physical attractiveness, or beauty

- wholeness

- health.

In his study of children over five years old, Richardson (1971) found that children in this age group devalue someone with an obvious impairment. He concluded from his research that:

'...society devalues all children with visible chronic impairments, and further, that a value hierarchy exists for children with chronic conditions based on type of impairment (i.e. visible or invisible) and relative attractiveness of impairment.'

ACTIVITY 10 ALLOW 15 MINUTES

Make a list of at least ten types of disability. (Don't worry about correct terminology at this stage.) Taking a personal view, which would you find less difficult and which would you find more difficult to cope with? Number your list in order, starting with 1 for least difficult, and so on.

Commentary

We cannot know which disabilities you included in your list. In ordering your preference, you may find that you have unconsciously created a list that relates well to the idea of condition visibility. The less visible a condition, the greater the extent to which an individual can mask that disability and pass as 'normal'. Most people are likely to feel that these disabilities would be easier to live with than those which are more visible. We discuss the reasons for this next.

Difference

Historically, defining difference was to some extent a means of ensuring safety, whether from outsiders, who could be an enemy, or from disease, which could threaten the whole social structure. With progress in the social and physical sciences, it has become possible to establish a high degree of refinement in the categorising or labelling of difference. In the developed world, certain categories have become extinct as diseases such as leprosy have been eradicated and, over time, the inclusive category of 'sameness' has become wider. But social structures have not yet evolved to the point where our fear of difference has been eradicated.

ACTIVITY 11 ALLOW 5 MINUTES

Think for a moment about your own social circle. What groups of people, situations or places make you feel uncomfortable because they are 'different'?

Commentary

Most of us expect to feel comfortable within our own family; indeed, the word family stems from the familiar, emphasising the associated sense of belonging. Entering unfamiliar territory is a major issue for many people. Think, for example, about entering a new sphere of work and the feelings of displacement that can occur in the new environment. A multi-course meal with a complex array of cutlery can produce feelings of insecurity about manners and etiquette. These examples from every-day life demonstrate the strength of our unconscious desire for familiarity.

We will now move on to examine some of the issues about language and attitudes relevant to the area of learning disability.

5: The power of language

During this century we can trace a growing social awareness of the negative nature of the language used to describe certain groups of people. The 1959 Mental Health Act acknowledged that medical and legal terminology which referred to people with a learning disability as 'imbeciles', 'idiots' and 'cretins' had become abusive. A change of language was seen as a positive move. The idea was that the new terms, which centred on 'subnormality', would be less negative. Other legislation in Scotland and America used the idea of 'retardation'. Twenty years later the 1980 Mental Health Act changed definitions, and so labels, yet again, also seeking a softer approach by using phrases such as 'mental impairment' and 'mental handicap'. Throughout this process, the abusive nature of language was recognised but the changing of terminology has failed to sensitise the public to the humanity of a group of people who are seen as very different.

Two key issues have arisen as a consequence of the continuing discussion around definitions and changing terminology.

1 Language alone cannot change attitudes if the people at the centre of the storm are regarded as less than human.

2 If the use of euphemistic language is seen as a reasonable alternative to positive action to reduce discrimination, people with disabilities will not achieve equal rights.

ACTIVITY 12 ALLOW 15 MINUTES

Read *Resource 3* in the *Resources Section*, an extract from Sinason (1992). Summarise in your own words two or three of the most important points she makes.

How far do you agree or disagree with Sinason's view that language change is a 'process of euphemism'?

Commentary

The key issues that Sinason raises are that:

- language changes do nothing for the groups involved and can be detrimental to progressing their cause

- there is a need to be aware of the difference between individual preference and group pressure in relation to the use of names and labels.

Sinason's arguments are persuasive. She suggests that there is a danger in 'progressive' language, in that the more remote the language from the impairment that determines the individual's status, the less those who label are likely to realise how their terminology maintains negative images. Sinason points out that the stigma associated with an intellectual impairment frequently transfers from one group of terms to the next: the actual terms do not alter relationships. She argues that language used over the past two or three decades has also tended to retain images of pity and poverty, which impair progress towards equal rights. Sinason also points out that if it becomes difficult to find the words to say what you mean, because you are afraid to use the wrong language, then it is possible that discourse in the area of learning disability could move from limited to absent. As she puts it, euphemism can mean that we become 'absolutely silent' about difficult issues.

The language of labels

Theories about language and disability tend to centre on the social construction of disability. The idea that disability is socially constructed can seem strange at first. It seems reasonable to say that the ability to walk exists or it does not; intellectual ability exists or it does not. Common sense tells us that these abilities are dependent on biological variables rather than social ones. However, the social construction theory requires us to move out of the arena of assumed 'truths' and reassess the nature of our environment. To do this we need to consider the nature of learning disability and whether or not this is defined in a way which has remained constant over time. We have seen that formal definitions or labels have changed, but have the boundaries which separate 'normal' intelligence from learning disability also moved over time?

ACTIVITY 13 — ALLOW 10 MINUTES

Can you think of at least six conditions which give rise to a disability or impairment? List them below.

When you have made your list, think back to the turn of the 20th century. To what extent has society's view of people affected by these conditions changed over the last 90 years?

Commentary

Your list may include some of the following:

- cerebral palsy
- deafness
- blindness
- Down's syndrome
- autism
- cerebrovascular accident
- trauma
- genetic or chromosomal abnormalities.

Today there is clearly a greater understanding of the nature of disability and its causes than there was at the turn of the century. For example, the individual who experienced deafness or autism would then have been regarded as a 'simple' person. The reason for this would have been linked to a single social criterion: the individual's ability to function as a contributing adult in that society. It was not until the early 1970s, for example, that it became generally recognised that some people with cerebral palsy could demonstrate the full range of intellectual functioning.

It seems that, in part at least, social knowledge does alter the way that disability is perceived and interpreted. The identification of whole groups of people as requiring special care has been linked to the historical moment of the industrial revolution. Walmsley (1994) writes:

'...some authors, notably Ryan and Thomas (1980) and Oliver (1990) argue that it was the introduction of factory-based work during the Industrial Revolution which led to disabled people being singled out as deviants requiring specialist facilities and medical treatment.'

Once a group of people (already regarded with some suspicion because they are in some way different) is removed from the community and crowded together behind walls, then labelling and the reinforcement of negative images becomes much easier. The next activity will help you to examine the significance of labelling in maintaining the undesirable image of people with a learning disability today.

ACTIVITY 14   ALLOW 10 MINUTES

Think about the colloquialisms used to describe people with a learning disability and write down as many as you can think of.

Commentary

It is possible that a truthful reflection on language in this exercise may have caused you some personal embarrassment. You may have noted words such as 'mongol', 'idiot', 'imbecile', 'spacker', 'phlid' (referring to thalidomide) and 'retard'. There are many others.

It is unnerving to find that words which are part of our every-day vocabulary have the potential to be as offensive as they are. When we describe ourselves as 'stupid', it is usually a reference to a single act rather than a label to describe our total being. If we think for a moment about the impact of language on our self-image, we may see more clearly the extent of the damage imposed by negative labels.

Once we realise that language can be abusive it is much easier to censor words than to analyse and change the social values underpinning that language.

6: Life chances and learning disability

Life chances: *The opportunities that are present in an individual's life.*

The diagnosis of learning disability and the ensuing labelling process has a profound impact upon the **life chances** of the individual. Like any other human condition, there are varying degrees of learning disability, ranging along a continuum from marginal impact to all-pervasive.

Specific and mild ——————————— Multiple
learning   intellectual/physical
disability   sensory disability

The following activity asks you to think about your own life chances and opportunities, before we move on to think about how these are shaped for people with a learning disability at both ends of the mild to severe continuum.

ACTIVITY 15 — ALLOW 10 MINUTES

Take a moment to think about your own life chances, past, present and future.

What are the features in your life which help or hinder you from achieving your potential?

What have been the important landmarks in your life?

Commentary

The features that you feel have influenced the positive aspects of your life may include things like family, education, employment, personal skills, strength of personality, disposition, or even luck. You may feel that you have been hindered by an unhappy family background, lack of education or perhaps bad luck. Most of us would like to feel that there is reasonable balance of opportunity and hindrance in our lives, although it is fair to say that life does seem easier for some than for others.

Your landmarks may have included things like exams passed at school or professional/work based qualifications. We can see life as a continuum along which we move with staged points or landmarks where we make choices or receive passports to the next stage. Linked to this idea of a continuum of life chances is the passage from childhood through adolescence to adulthood. For many people the important landmarks in this passage may be things like choosing certain friends or social activities, falling in love, deciding to leave home, becoming financially independent, finding a partner, or having children.

The emphasis on creating opportunities for people with learning disabilities tends to be placed at the milder end of the ability range. This not surprising, as the ability to articulate needs and opinions is highly valued in our culture. The absence of a physical voice, when combined with a stigmatising condition, can lead to a loss of presence in society. Opportunity for personal growth is linked in part to individual potential, but the environment in which a person develops has a significant influence on the extent to which that potential can be realised. Atkinson and Williams (1990) quote a young man with learning disabilities talking about his work in an Adult Training Centre:

'There's plenty of things we could do but we don't get the chance. The only one thing that's stopping us really is working in here and we're labelled and that's what 'cos I hate being in here. If you're in here you get labelled as handicapped.'

This young man feels that he has no life opportunities, that other people in his social sphere regard him as handicapped first, and that they rarely if ever see him as an able person. The label 'handicapped' is rejected because of the limitations it imposes upon him and because it does not describe him as he sees himself.

Many of our individual successes depend upon the esteem that significant people give us. While it may be flattering to think of ourselves as hard-working and self-determining, the reality is that opportunities are frequently offered on the basis of assumptions about ability rather than ability itself. Think back to any job interview, for example, and you will be aware that your outward appearance and presentation were carefully thought through to show yourself in your best light. People with a handicap that is visible at first sight or in early conversation find that negative assumptions are made about their ability on the basis of their appearance. They are not often given opportunities that will develop their potential, because prejudicial barriers are raised by powerful others. A person with a mild learning disability may suffer more from the consequences of prejudice, imposed limitations on life chances, and the constraints of unthinking support services, than from the disability itself.

We will now consider the perspective of a person with severe learning disabilities.

ACTIVITY 16 — ALLOW 10 MINUTES

> Lena is 35 years old. She experienced trauma at birth causing damage to her brain. She greets her mother in the morning with a smile and some vocalising that can indicate pleasure, need, pain or displeasure. Her parents are now retired and find that at last they have the space in their lives necessary to care for her. Lena cannot walk or sit unsupported, and needs help with almost every aspect of living. She seems to be happy.

Note down four or five ways in which Lena's disabilities shape her life chances. (You may want to do this by comparing her abilities and life chances with those of the young man considered above.)

Commentary

In Lena's case you are likely to have noted the absence of social ability. Her lack of a voice that would be understood by strangers creates many limitations in her life and prevents her demonstrating her potential. Lena can indicate feelings, but her disabilities mean that other people know very little about *what* she feels, thinks, or is conscious of.

At the age of thirty-five, Lena is still living with and dependent upon her parents. She cannot make her wishes known and is reliant on those who provide her care to truly understand her. Complete physical dependence on others can result in the status of 'child' becoming lifelong. You may have come across the phrase 'eternal child' used in this context.

The impact of learning disability is dependent upon the degree of intellectual impairment and on the social interpretation of that ability, which influences the lifestyle of the individual.

ACTIVITY 17   ALLOW 20 MINUTES

Read *Resource 4* in the *Resources Section*, an extract from Gerald Sanctuary's book *After I'm Gone What Will Happen to My Handicapped Child?* How do Arthur and Moira's stories link in to the discussions in this session?

1 Choose from the extract some examples of language which devalues the potential or actual abilities of people with disabilities.

2 The extract describes major landmarks or life chances in Moira and Arthur's lives. What were they? What were other people's initial reactions to the opportunities that Moira and Arthur wanted to pursue?

3 Summarise the effects of Moira and Arthur's disabilities on other members of their family.

4 How did Arthur's siblings regard him? How did their attitudes and responses to him change over time? Why did they change?

Commentary

Although Arthur and Moira had different kinds of disability, their experience of life was limited by prejudice and its potential to create further barriers and limitations in their lives. Refer back to the text in the session if you need help in relating your notes to the session objectives.

Summary

1 In this session we have examined some causes of learning disability and explored four common associated conditions.

2 We have initiated your learning about the concept and experience of learning disability.

3 The impact of the birth of a child with a learning disability upon parents and siblings has been explored.

4 We have highlighted the way language both reflects social values about learning disability and influences the social status of people with a learning disability.

Before you move on to Session Two, check that you have achieved the learning objectives given at the beginning of this session and, if not, review the appropriate sections.

The history and development of services for people with a learning disability

Introduction

This session explores past and present influences upon the provision of health and social care for people with a learning disability. Its focus is upon the history of the social construction of learning disability. The first part of the session takes the form of an historical review of attitudes and approaches to care. The second part focuses upon the developments that have arisen from the inception of the mixed economy of care.

Session objectives

When you have completed this session you should be able to:

- review the history of care for people with learning disabilities and relate this to the prevailing attitudes of the time

- describe the impact of institutionalisation on individual development

- explain the current structure of care provision and the significance of the mixed economy of care.

1: The historical antecedents to present day care

To understand the way our present services have developed, it is helpful to review how society's understanding of disability and difference has developed over time. We start by delving into some of the meanings that disability has been given at different points in history, and relate this to past approaches to care.

ACTIVITY 18   ALLOW 5 MINUTES

Think back to Session One which described some of the ways in which individuals with the label 'learning disability' and their families experience difference. Can you recall at least two or three ways in which society makes them feel different?

Commentary

Language was one of the main issues we explored. You may have mentioned the use of negative language and its impact on the self-esteem of the individual. We also discussed the way social values shape people's experience of disability. You may have mentioned condition visibility and the tendency to make negative assumptions about an individual's ability on the basis of appearance alone; the shared stigma experienced by other family members; and the way in which other people's conscious or unconscious prejudices limit the life chances of disabled people.

It is possible to trace over time two broad strands or divisions in definitions of difference. These are the inhuman and the animal-like. We will examine each theme in turn before moving to more recent times. Our particular concern in this part of the session is the unconscious impact of history upon the present. An exploration of past understandings and treatment of people considered different will help to answer the question of where our present fears of difference originate.

Inhuman?

Early thinkers sought explanations for different appearances in the human form. These explanations took the form of rationalisations that different people were something other than human.

One view was that the hand of God had touched these 'poor souls', rendering them 'holy innocents' who should be segregated from the rest of humanity, lest other mere mortals should contaminate their holy state. This was a common medieval view, exemplified in Bosch's painting *Stultifara Navis* or *Ship of Fools*, which depicts a ship of different-appearing people on a sea journey. Foucault (1965) writes extensively about this and takes the 'Ship of Fools' as the title of his first chapter.

ACTIVITY 19 — ALLOW 5 MINUTES

Why do you think people in the early middle ages took the view that difference came from the hand of God?

Commentary

In medieval Europe, religious belief was of a literal nature. God was as real to the ordinary person of that period as images sent by satellite are to us today. Physical or mental deviations from the norm were seen as manifestations of God's will, with a divine purpose. Although this purpose must not be questioned, there still existed feelings of disquiet. Reasoning that such God-touched people should be excluded was a way of dealing with these feelings of discomfort. (The psychological term for such feelings is 'dissonance'.)

Another view was that the devil's influence made people into parodies of the human state. This view of evil as a malignant influence on humanity is the most enduring of the three strands of belief which sought to explain deformity and difference. Whilst I do not suggest that this is an acceptable view, it is understandable that difference was more readily perceived as something negative than positive, and therefore linked to evil rather than to good.

ACTIVITY 20 — ALLOW 5 MINUTES

Even today, children growing up in our society are exposed to ideas and images which suggest that difference, particularly that linked with disability, may be associated with evil. Can you think of some examples?

Commentary

From an early age we may learn at an unconscious level to link beauty with goodness and ugliness with evil, or at least with 'badness'. Children's fairy stories combine beauty and goodness in the physical form of heroes and heroines, who have to prove themselves against adversaries such as wicked witches, evil trolls or goblins. You may have thought of stories like *Treasure Island* or *Peter Pan*, where the anti-hero or villain has some form of disability. (The work of Colin Barnes (1992) provides further insight into this issue.)

The devil himself is often represented with a deformed or abnormal human shape. Young children are easily frightened by unfamiliar features, or someone wearing a mask. This fear can be amplified by parents' cautionary tales of bogey men. Watch TV advertisements for a few days and notice how many of them exploit or parody these attitudes and fears.

At an unconscious level, then, it seems that present day society as a whole retains many early mystical ideas linking good with beauty and bad with difference or ugliness. Right up until the mid 1960s, a physical condition typified by extended growth of the facial bones was referred to in respected medical texts as 'gargoylism'. Gargoyles are ugly stone effigies which medieval stonemasons placed at the corners of church roofs to frighten away other evil spirits.

A third view of difference, documented in the sixteenth and seventeenth centuries, was that it was not the direct influence of God and the devil, but the work of witches or lesser spirits such as fairies, who would leave a changeling in exchange for a perfect human baby which they had stolen away. To someone living in the twentieth century this sounds far-fetched, but this view has its own rationale.

ACTIVITY 21   ALLOW 10 MINUTES

What might make the idea of the changeling credible in a pre-scientific age? What physical evidence might give parents cause to believe that some form of exchange of babies had occurred?

Commentary

Think about a baby born with cerebral palsy, hydrocephalus, or any other condition which only becomes visible in the period after birth. At birth, this baby seems perfect to the untutored eye. It is only much later that the child with cerebral palsy may develop obvious contractures of the limbs. Similarly, the enlargement of the skull associated with hydrocephalus only becomes apparent over a period of time. Parents naturally sought some explanation for the seemingly drastic changes in their child which appeared to have developed overnight. Their knowledge of the world was based on religious and superstitious belief. Things that could not be explained in any other way had to be the work of God, the devil, witchcraft or the lesser order of mischievous and sometimes evil sprites thought to prey on humankind. It was easy to blame a spiteful fairy for stealing a perfect human child in exchange for a deformed fairy child. In the seventeenth century the term 'changeling' actually came to mean 'fool' or 'imbecile'.

'Changelings' were dealt with in ways that echo into the present. The baby was reviled and the 'other', beautiful, perfect baby was missed and needed back in the family home. The 'changeling' was returned to the fairy world by leaving it on the hillside or in the forest, so that the spirits would see their child and accept the exchange.

ACTIVITY 22 — ALLOW **10** MINUTES

Can you think of other myths or stories about children abandoned in the wild? What subsequently happened to them?

Commentary

You may have thought of the story of Romulus and Remus, the founders of Rome, who according to legend were abandoned as babies and then brought up by a she-wolf. This is an idea found in a number of other myths and stories, but more contemporary are the stories of 'wolf children' which began to emerge in the eighteenth century. These include supposedly true accounts of children, found almost fully grown, living wild and thought to have been brought up by wolves or other wild animals. Although far from common, cases of wild or feral children continue to be uncovered today.

The changeling idea does not account for all such children. It is likely that isolated peasants or foresters died and left children who had to fend for themselves. There is no evidence that wild animals adopt children. However, children who were old enough to forage but too young to have social skills might survive. Anthropological studies such as that by Turnbull (1980) indicate that abandoned children can survive from a surprisingly young age.

There may be a link between the idea of abandoned 'changelings' and early stories of feral children. Thus, in the eighteenth century stories, children who were different and at one time seen as 'inhuman' (changelings), became 'animal-like' (wolf-children).

Animal-like?

Let us move on to consider the emergence of the asylum, and its later consequences. Bedlam, given by Henry VIII to the City of London as a 'hospital for lunatics' in 1547, is perhaps the most famous, or infamous, asylum in this country. It housed many types of people who were 'different', all sharing the common stigma which kept them bound and sometimes chained within its walls. Conditions in the asylum reflected the attitudes of the time towards people who were different. The mad and deformed were classed as animal-like, thought to require no human comforts but needing to be constrained lest they harm others.

ACTIVITY 23	ALLOW 15 MINUTES

What kind of facilities for food, hygiene and physical care would you expect to find in an asylum where people were regarded as animals? Try to imagine at least three or four features of the physical environment. Note them down and then make notes on how each feature might help to promote or reinforce the view that inmates were indeed like animals.

Commentary

Below are the dehumanising features I thought of, but your list may well include others:

● an absence of furniture, requiring people to sit or lie on the floor

● minimal clothing and a high incidence of nakedness

● limited hygiene facilities, so that people were dirty, unkempt and foul-smelling

● food served in troughs or even on the floor, forcing people to eat at ground level

● the use of iron chains to bind, provoking resistance and perhaps even ferocity.

You may have recognised that the more an individual is treated like an animal, the less likely it becomes that any humanising behaviour will emerge.

The condition of madness or physical or intellectual difference would add its own barrier to seeing the person as a human being rather than an 'inmate'. We know from historical accounts that asylum inmates were harshly and at times brutally treated. The use of iron waistcoats to restrain individuals into cramped positions is recorded (Scull, 1979).

The attendants or caretakers of Bedlam supplemented their income by providing public tours of the asylum. Inmates became the focus of freak shows, where deformity and difference were captured within barred cages and displayed for public scrutiny and ridicule in exchange for money. The process of shutting people away in asylums or hospitals then resulted, paradoxically, in the increase in their social visibility, as the asylums acquired notoriety among the population at large.

In the eighteenth century, enlightened thinkers came to regard the asylum as a place of horror and major reforms were proposed. Two key figures were Tuke in England and Pinel in France. William Tuke's concern about conditions in the York County Asylum, for example, persuaded the Society of Quakers to finance the founding of a new hospital in 1791. Named The Retreat, it is one of the most famous hospitals in the history of learning disability. It became famous for its humane treatment of the mentally disturbed and was the precursor to the 'Reform Movement for Lunacy'.

The work of these reformers represented a watershed: from this point the dehumanisation of vulnerable people was challenged and more positive regimes proposed. Eighteenth century reforms were limited, however, by the scientific understanding of the time. Thus, although there developed some idea of differentiation between the many types of condition that had until then been collectively labelled 'different' or 'lunatic' (Foucault, 1965), within the field of mental health the notion of 'curable' and 'incurable' emerged. It was recognised that some people could benefit from education and others could not: the 'educable' and 'ineducable'. In the late eighteenth century, Itard established a school for feral children to investigate whether they could benefit from education.

Thus the end of the eighteenth century represents a period of transition in our belief systems, where conflicting sets of ideas meet. The inhuman and the animal-like merge in these feral children, left in the wild because they were perhaps thought to be changelings, now being schooled for the purposes of research.

The distinction between educable or ineducable groups of stigmatised people continued into the nineteenth and early twentieth centuries, and has repercussions even today. The right to education was established by the 1870 Education Act but this did not apply to children with special needs, who were excluded from the mainstream system. It was not until relatively recently that access to mainstream education for people with a learning disability was established. Before this, schools which catered for children with learning disabilities were mainly attached to large hospitals rather than to the education system; they were also largely run by unqualified staff.

2: The modern institution

The reform of the large asylums in the eighteenth century seemed to point towards a positive future and the development of better care provision. People who were visibly different, and who experienced learning difficulties which impeded their ability to function in society, were helped in more humane ways. But social events in the second half of the nineteenth and early twentieth century significantly impeded this progress.

Darwin published his *Origin of the Species* in 1859. His theory of natural selection was then extrapolated by some Victorian thinkers into social theories to justify the 'survival of the fittest' (or more exactly, the extinction of the unfit) in human society. *Social Darwinism* suggested that if the 'feeble-minded' in society were allowed to breed then the nation's gene pool would be diluted and the future health of the population threatened.

ACTIVITY 24   ALLOW 15 MINUTES

What reaction might you expect from a society which believed the predictions of social Darwinism to be correct?

What developments might be expected in provision for people with learning disabilities?

What other groups of people might be regarded as 'unfit' to breed?

Commentary

Social Darwinism engendered a widespread fear of over-breeding by so-called 'feeble minded' people, and precipitated the preparation of new hospitals to lock away people who were diagnosed as having some intellectual impairment. These hospitals served to protect society from the polluting effects of people referred to as imbeciles, cretins and idiots. Fear of, and the need to contain, these polluting elements effectively arrested the progress towards more humanising forms of care.

Fear of contamination spread into a wider moral panic and those people who were regarded as promiscuous or degenerate were also locked away. Men and women in Victorian institutions were kept strictly apart, lest they develop promiscuous behaviours which could threaten wider society. The segregation of men and women remained normal practice until the 1970s and even then was only reluctantly discontinued (Jones, 1972).

Large institutions continued to thrive well into the middle of the twentieth century. Our historical review helps us to understand why it took so long for the public and politicians to begin to question the value of these institutions. The moral panic which powered the building of the Victorian institutions also prevented the ordinary citizen from questioning the harshness of the care regime. People were labelled 'defective' because they could not function as members of society and because their reproduction posed the threat of genetic pollution.

The power of these arguments may seem to have justified the terrible nature of the institution. The idea that the disability was permanent, or incurable, added to this fear and exacerbated the poor treatment of people with a disability.

Putting people away in institutions removed them from public sight. The public became unused to seeing, let alone discussing, these kind of differences. So the fear of difference also became a fear of the unseen and unknown.

3: Institutionalisation

If you look up the word 'institution' in a dictionary you will find it refers to '[an] organisation founded especially for charitable, religious, educational or social purposes' and to 'established law or custom'. The word 'institutionalised' has a much more sinister meaning: 'made apathetic and dependent after a long period in an institution' (Oxford English Dictionary, 1995). **Institutionalisation** refers to the way in which the organisation of care totally controls the life of the person receiving that care.

Some of the key ideas which inform our understanding of institutionalisation come from the work of Erving Goffman, an American sociologist, who published *Asylums* in 1961. It was Goffman who coined the phrase **'total institution'**, referring to the impact the institution has upon every aspect of the life of the inmate.

Institutionalisation: *The debilitating impact of life in a total institution, leading to loss of self identity and personal power.*

Total institution: *A place of residence and work where a large number of like situated individuals, cut off from the wider society for an appreciable period, together lead an enclosed, formally administered round of life.*

ACTIVITY 25	ALLOW 25 MINUTES

Read the extract from *Asylums, Resource 5* in the *Resources Section*, using a dictionary to check any terms you don't understand. Then try and summarise in your own words the ten elements of institutionalisation that Goffman describes.

Commentary

Compare your summary with mine. The elements that Goffman identifies are:

1 There is a breakdown of the barriers which separate the various spheres of social life: play, sleep, and work.

2 All aspects of life occur in the same environment.

3 All aspects of life are controlled by a single authority.

4 Daily activities are experienced in conjunction with many other people, who are treated similarly and are subject to the same timetable.

5 All aspects of daily life are managed through a rigid and tightly structured timetable.

6 The timetable is imposed by those in authority; the subject has no influence or power in determining personal daily needs.

7 This rigid structure forms part of a rational plan which seeks to fulfil the aim of the institution.

8 There exist two groups of people in the institution, inmates and supervisory staff.

9 These two groups of people regard each other with mutual hostility and in negative terms.

10 The staff are seen by inmates as owning the institution and being in control. The work of the staff frequently benefits themselves rather than inmates.

These features of the total institution give us insight into the ways that a few staff can achieve the submission of many inmates. The first stage in this submission is the process through which inmates pass as they enter the institution. The next activity examines the process of becoming an inmate.

ACTIVITY 26   ALLOW 25 MINUTES

Read the extract from Morgan et al. (1985) *Resource 6* in the *Resources Section*. (This is a secondary source, as it is another writer's interpretation of Goffman's work.) Write a short explanation of each of the terms below in your own words. Include in your explanation some examples of each process in practice.

Mortification of the self

Reorganisation of the self

Patient response

Colonisation

Conversion

Withdrawn

Intransigent

Commentary

Mortification of the self. To mortify the self literally means 'to deaden' or 'to destroy the vital functions of' the self. This involves the degradation of the person, through the removal of those factors that create a sense of individuality. For example, taking away personal clothing, or having to request permission to do something that adults normally decide for themselves, such as smoking a cigarette or getting a drink of coffee. The admission ritual of bathing the 'dirty' individual under supervision creates humiliation, as hygiene is regarded as private and personal in our culture.

Reorganisation of the self. The hospital gives the degraded self a new identity by using hospital uniform, requiring the adoption of the role of the patient, and substituting the hospital's social network for the individual's former social life. Each new inmate experiences this process differently, but ultimately the balance of power in the system limits the scope for reaction.

Patient response. The way in which patients react to their role in the institution. Three types of response are described:

- **colonisation**: the inmate can accept the process of submission, but unwillingly (like the indigenous peoples of countries which are colonised by foreign powers)

- **conversion**: over time, some inmates assimilate their new identity and become positively reconciled to their role as patient

- **withdrawn** or **intransigent**: patients who reject the system may either give up hope and retreat into themselves, or become very difficult. You may have worked with clients who responded to their care by being compliant to the point of invisibility. You may recall others whose extreme reactions and absence of compliance created problems for the organisation, and got them the label 'problem patient'.

Barton (1976) suggests that eight key factors in the environment are associated with *institutional neurosis*.

ACTIVITY 27 — ALLOW 25 MINUTES

Read *Resource 7* in the *Resources Section*, an extract from Barton's *Institutional Neurosis*. According to Barton, which of the eight environmental factors has the most serious effect on patients?

Commentary

You will note that Barton says he has amended the list of factors that appeared in the first edition, because he has come to recognise that 'violence, brutality, bullying, browbeating, harshness, teasing and tormenting' are far more common than he had realised, and probably the most powerful factor in subjugating patients.

The extracts you have read by Barton and Morgan describe some important features of twentieth century care institutions. Physical conditions and ideas about acceptable forms of treatment have clearly progressed since the early asylums, however, you may have been struck by similarities between the harshness of the environment, the humiliation, loss of identity, bullying and brutality of twentieth century institutions and the characteristics of Bedlam that we explored earlier. Modern society is, in many ways, more humane, but in our own terms, institutionalisation is a relatively inhumane and dehumanising way to care for people. It is startling that someone like Barton, working within the system, failed for so long to see that it brutalises inmates. To brutalise means literally 'to make like a brute or animal', which reminds us that echoes of past attitudes are still with us in the present.

ACTIVITY 28 — ALLOW 10 MINUTES

In the extract in *Resource 7*, Barton says 'I am amazed and humiliated that with all the evidence given me by patients, relatives and staff – especially those I was treating – I did not identify and record it [brutality] years ago'.

Why do you think the brutality of the institution remained invisible to an intelligent and caring person like Barton? Write down at least two or three reasons why people who work in a care environment may become blind to poor practice.

Commentary

We have suggested four reasons. You may well have thought of other factors which contribute to an inability to see poor practice or unacceptable conditions.

- Survival in the workplace often depends on the strange very rapidly becoming familiar and routine.

- Because many people unconsciously learn in childhood that those who are visibly different are somehow less civilised or less human, this makes it easier to see the barren nature of the institutional care environment as normal. If incontinence did not exist then the smell of urine would not permeate the air: in other words, the part played by staff in creating incontinence or poor living conditions goes undetected if the blame is laid consciously or unconsciously on the person who is incontinent.

- If individuals have limited communication skills, either as a result of their disability or of limitations imposed by the environment, professional carers become used to listening to themselves, or others like themselves. Listening to clients is not the norm.

- Professionals may be blind because, quite simply, if an incident comes to their attention that offends their sensibilities, it is easier to treat it as unbelievable.

French (1994) highlights the paradox in this final point:

> 'One of the reasons that abuse of disabled people, both inside and outside institutions, remains undiscovered, is that many people have difficulty believing it exists, whereas in reality, disabled people appear to be at greater risk from abuse than others.'

Poor care is not a thing of the past. We have to recognise that present day care services have a history and carry with them some of the prejudices of that history. Only recently, a staff member in a small home for profoundly handicapped children was found to have mistreated and abused the children. Parents had experienced great difficulty in getting the senior officers of the local authority to take seriously and investigate their complaints of ill-treatment. There are other examples of people with learning disabilities making complaints of physical or sexual abuse in health and social care settings. Their complaints were discounted because they were considered to have poor reasoning abilities and to be unreliable witnesses. Further reading in this area is available in Westcott (1994) and Bannister (1992).

We are now in a position to review what has been learned so far. From early times, stigma has attached to people with learning disabilities. Throughout history this has reinforced by and reflected in the power of negative language and labelling. Much later, pseudo-scientific arguments fuelled existing prejudice and fear, and justified the segregation of these people from the rest of society. This segregation served to reinforce the devaluing of people with learning disabilities.

4: Community care and the mixed economy

The definition of disability, and in particular of mental handicap and mental illness, as a medical problem legitimised the removal of a large number of people from wider society. Segregation was achieved by the systematic removal of disabled people from their homes and local communities. In many cases the doctor advised parents to forget about their child once he or she was admitted to hospital. This strategy quietly removed the sole natural advocates usually available to children – their parents. Since the 1959 Mental Health Act there has been a growing voice for the movement of care provision away from the institution into the community. The debate has emphasised the social nature of disability, and especially learning disability, as opposed to the biological nature of the underlying impairment. The 'cure' for low social value is seen to lie outside the institution within society at large. *Resource 8* lists the reports and legislation which have moved policy in this direction over the past few decades.

ACTIVITY 29　　　　　ALLOW 5 MINUTES

Learning disability is viewed as a problem in some societies and not in others (Edgerton, 1976). Below is a list of factors which may encourage people to see learning disability as a problem in our society. Which do you think are the most significant?

- hospitals for people with learning disabilities were geographically isolated

- people need far more sophisticated skills for daily living today than 100 years ago

- learning disability is medically diagnosed and managed, and so seen as a medical problem

- limited educational opportunities do not enable people to achieve their full potential

- people who are not literate are not valued in a society which values literacy

- negative language reflects and reinforces negative social attitudes to learning disability.

Commentary

You may have found it difficult to say which factors are the most significant in the social construction of learning disability and to some extent they are interdependent. If a group of people is socially and geographically isolated and denied educational opportunities, they are less likely to develop skills for daily living or sophisticated literacy skills, or to achieve their full potential in any other sphere. As long as their condition is regarded as an 'incurable' medical problem this situation is unlikely to change.

In considering the list of factors, it may also have struck you that people can lead successful lives without literacy skills, and that some aspects of daily living are considerably easier today than they were fifty or a hundred years ago. These need not be insurmountable obstacles, but if people with learning disabilities are segregated, wider society remains ignorant of their needs, potential and aspirations. Prejudice and negative stereotypes thrive on this ignorance.

ACTIVITY 30 · ALLOW 10 MINUTES

1 What are the advantages of care in a community setting for people with learning a disability? Note down at least two or three ways in which this policy may help to tackle some of the issues discussed in the last activity.

2 Are there disadvantages? Note down any you can think of.

Commentary

1 We thought of two important advantages. You can probably add others. The integration of people into community settings means that the individual is removed from the constraints of the hospital environment, and given opportunities to develop wider experiences of life, and skills for living. Second, the process of accepting people as people first requires 'community presence': in other words, the presence in the community of people with a learning disability serves to educate the public. This presence may eventually remove many of the deep-rooted fears which sustain stigma and prejudice.

2 There are disadvantages if the implementation of this policy is not thought through with care. Some people argue that the 'community presence' approach is ill-advised and even immoral and that people with a learning disability should not have to function as educators of the public. It is also important to realise that institutionalisation is not determined by size alone. The term '**micro-institutionalisation**' is used to describe the impact of power and control on the lives of people in small care settings. All sectors of the care services realise the potential for abuse that is inherent in providing care: there have been examples in the health and

Micro-institutionalisation: *The impact of a lifestyle within a small residential home in the community that is similar to the consequences of the very negative environment evident in the large hospital.*

social services, and in private and voluntary agencies. In establishing community care as a positive force for the future, a priority must be the development of effective safeguards against abuse.

The development of the 1990 Community Care Act gave impetus to the development of innovative community care services for people with learning disabilities. It required local authorities to purchase a proportion of care services from the independent sector, so creating a **mixed economy of care**.

The private sector

As community care became a reality, the private sector expanded. There was a marked increase in the number of small, privately-owned home-style developments, housing three to five people. These provided a pattern for development throughout all care sectors, public and voluntary as well as private.

In the early days of community care, benefit levels gave the individual enough income to pay for private care on transfer from a long-stay hospital. The benefit structure has since changed, so that, in real terms, individuals have less money available to pay for care. This has created financial difficulties, forcing some homes to sell up or close. Owners sometimes advertise homes for sale complete with 'nice' occupants. When a home is sold, the new owner is at liberty to change the client group, and existing occupants may have to move elsewhere.

> **Mixed economy of care:** *The delivery of care involving the public, private and voluntary sectors that crosses the boundaries of health and social services.*

ACTIVITY 31   ALLOW 5 MINUTES

Imagine you are a tenant living in privately rented accommodation. How does your situation differ from that of the private care home residents described above?

Commentary

As a tenant you are likely to have a rent book. This automatically gives you certain rights, which are clearly not available to the residents of care homes. Although small homes may give people greater control over their day-to-day lives on one level, residents still have little real control over decisions about where they will live. Of course, voluntary and public sector care homes may close or change their nature, but competition among private sector care homes tends to increase the level of insecurity for private residents.

There is much that is positive in the arena of private care. The extent to which it will result in positive experiences at the individual level, however, will be determined by the extent to which people have personal control over the care they receive. We shall return to one area in which greater control can be achieved at the end of the session.

The voluntary sector

When the community care reforms were first proposed, the charitable foundations were keen to develop services. The best known charitable and non-profit making organisations in the field of learning disability are Mencap, Dr. Barnardo's and Scope. They wanted to establish residential, domiciliary and day-care services that would avoid the pitfalls they had criticised in health and social services provision. Voluntary sector bodies also provided much needed community-based housing through housing associations and sheltered housing schemes. Many of these enterprises have flourished and provide models of good practice.

ACTIVITY 32 ALLOW **10** MINUTES

Reflect for a moment on the traditional role of charities such as Mencap. Can you see any conflict between the old and new roles? Note down your thoughts below.

Commentary

Many charities have traditionally been watchdogs, campaigners and advocates in circles of power, lobbying politicians and policy-makers to ensure that services improve. In their new role as providers, some charities find that they are in conflict with these original aims. They have come face to face with the difficulties of providing care services within a limited budget. Their role is now divided – and therefore weakened in the eyes of some.

Public sector: social services

The community care legislation required local authority social services departments to become lead authorities for the development of **community care** services. Social services departments were required to purchase a proportion of care from the private and voluntary sectors rather than providing most services themselves. In order to monitor the quality of these developing services, the government required that social services departments undertake the inspection of independent sector residential homes, and develop care management arrangements.

Community care:
The provision of care within local communities, usually in 'ordinary' housing, such as small residential homes, or within the family.

Linked to this, the reforms also required the development of greater co-operation between the various care agencies. It is common to find that health and social services combine their strengths, particularly in the provision of domiciliary services. Community teams for people with a learning disability frequently consist of social workers, community nurses and psychology assistants.

There is, however, some dissent about the most appropriate format for future service provision. In many cases, people with a learning disability require very individual forms of help, while services are commonly geared to broad categories such as ambulant or non-ambulant clients, clients with good social skills, or clients with challenging behaviour. This observation is common to all service providers, but it is social services departments who are responsible for purchasing services from other providers. They may decide on a purchasing strategy which tends to maintain the existing pattern of services, or which develops innovative and more individual forms of care.

ACTIVITY 33   ALLOW 10 MINUTES

How are care services for adults with a learning disability organised in your area? List the broad categories or types of service that you are aware of. Your list should include health, social services, and private and voluntary services.

Commentary

The organisation of services varies widely from area to area, but compare your list with mine, which covers a range of services provided by different agencies:

- services for profoundly physically and intellectually impaired people
- special units for people who exhibit challenging behaviour
- provision for those with a moderate disability
- provision for older people with a learning disability
- services for people with a '**dual diagnosis**' of learning disability and mental illness.

The categories of services in your area may look somewhat different, but this activity has perhaps made you aware that the broad divisions in the traditional pattern of services do not always make it easy to tailor care to individual needs.

Dual diagnosis: *The presence of two diagnosed conditions usually referring to the combined diagnosis of learning disability and mental health problems.*

Public sector: the health service

The greater the severity of a person's impairment and resulting handicap, the more likely it is that their care will be provided in the health service, where provision has focused on the areas of challenging behaviour, dual diagnosis, and a secure environment. (There is some development of hospital services in the private sector. It is worth noting Goffman's warning that if the institution was closed down, people in power would seek to reopen it in some other guise.) Health service hospitals for people with a learning disability are closing down and being replaced by services in the community. Some excellent community services are emerging, particularly in the area of dual diagnosis, but at the same time the need for a limited amount of care in a controlled environment has also been recognised.

In the field of health care, one branch of nursing specialises in the care of people with a learning disability. With the development of community care, these nurses may be trained throughout the care sector, in public, private or voluntary agencies. The Department of Health has made a commitment to maintaining this training. For many this is seen as good news, as vulnerable people with nursing needs have every right to receive this care from a knowledgeable and competent practitioner. There is, however, an opposing view, which argues the need for people with a learning disability to have greater access to 'ordinary' or mainstream services. Specialised nursing can be seen as a way of maintaining segregation, so reducing the contact with other services that would help to break down the fears and reservations of other professionals and the public.

ACTIVITY 34

ALLOW 5 MINUTES

In this session I have pointed out that learning disability can be seen as socially determined, or as a medically diagnosed condition. Work through the key words and phrases in the box below. Underline those which you think best fit in with the medical model of learning disability, and circle those which fit in with the view that it is socially determined.

reduce or remove the limitations imposed by other people

treatment in hospital

help to develop potential

support from a team of professionals

make opportunities to achieve aspirations

patient has a learning disability

consultant treats the condition   change social attitudes

care in a home-like environment

client suffers from intellectual impairment

Commentary

You may have found some of these ideas easier to categorise than others. The most significant difference between a medical and a social description of learning disability is that the former locates the condition firmly within the individual, and focuses on treatment rather than care and support. The social model recognises that external factors in the physical and social environment help to create and maintain limitations. Using these guiding principles you should be able to decide which of the ideas above belong firmly to one view or the other, and which might belong to both.

Health service provision has traditionally focused on the medical model of learning disability, but some services are recognising the limitations of this. The use of the term 'client' rather than 'patient' in some areas of nursing, for example, acknowledges that the relationship between the practitioner and the person needing care should be a helping one, not a controlling one. With the development of community care and increased joint working between health and social services, these sharp differences in understanding and approaches may become more blurred.

5: Looking forward

To be successful, community care developments must recognise the need to tackle the negative attitudes of the public and, in some cases, of other professionals. This seems a good idea, but how can it be achieved in practice? What part can the individual practitioner play? In this final part of the session we will consider the idea of the **vicious circle** and of the **virtuous circle**. O'Brien and Tyne (1981) use the idea of a vicious circle to explain the continuation of negative social values within a social group. They suggest that these values can be reversed through the use of a **virtuous circle**.

Vicious circle:
A series of life events that start from a negative assumption about the potential of an individual and lead towards the degradation of ability: a self-fulfilling prophecy.

Virtuous circle:
The antithesis of a vicious circle in that a skill or positive attribute of an individual is highlighted, so leading to further positive life experiences.

ACTIVITY 35	ALLOW 25 MINUTES

1　Read the extract from O'Brien and Tyne, *Resource 9* in the *Resources Section*.

2　Think of someone you know who may have experienced this kind of negative cycle. Draw your own diagram of what that person's vicious circle might look like.

3　Draw a virtuous circle that could help to promote self-belief and an ability to learn.

Vicious circle

Virtuous circle

Commentary

I selected a young man called Ian who I met when he lived in a 'pre-discharge' unit. He was learning self-care skills, so that he could move from the large hospital to a small hostel or a flat of his own. He was introduced to me by other personnel as lazy, dirty and useless. I felt that such an introduction could have long-term repercussions for his future. Ian's vicious circle appears in *Figure 2* below and his virtuous circle in *Figure 3*.

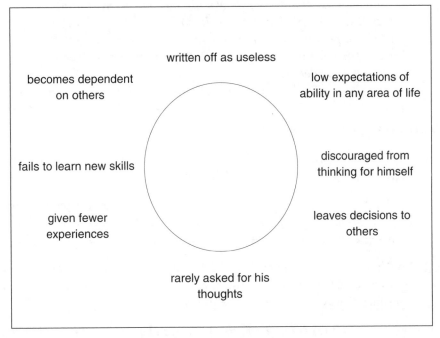

Figure 2: Ian's vicious circle

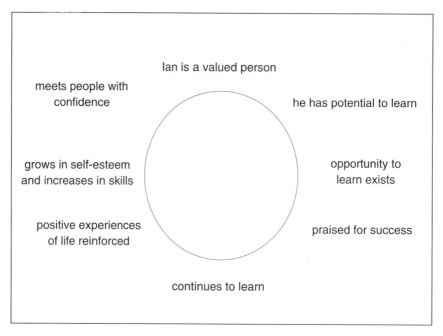

Figure 3: Ian's virtuous circle

Giving people greater control over their care?

People with disabilities want to be given control of the finances that procure services. The People First movement provides a coherent voice for people with learning disabilities, for whom this is also an issue. There are many who are unable fully to articulate their needs, but who have a voice through their advocates. The words of disabled people themselves should bring this session to a close.

> 'Instead of giving us rights, the Community Care Act puts us in the Limboland of uncertainty between a mixed market place of providers on the one hand, and professional controllers of services on the other. ...The right-wing view of the market place as the source of meeting our needs is as hopeless and redundant as the hope that they will somehow be met through the state-controlled system of democratic accountability – which in practice is accountable not to us, but the infinitely more powerful interest groups which feed on our artificially created dependency.'
>
> (Derbyshire Coalition of Disabled People 1993)

Summary

1 In this session we have considered historical beliefs, attitudes and myths surrounding people exhibiting difference.

2 We have explored the development of institutional care for people with a learning disability and looked at the way the asylum became the means of their segregation from the general population.

3 You have begun to develop an understanding of the way present day services emerged and why the term 'mixed economy of care' is an appropriate way of describing these services.

Before you move on to Session Three, check that you have achieved the objectives given at the beginning of this session and, if not, review the appropriate sections.

SESSION THREE

Normalisation

Introduction

This session explores the concept of normalisation through a review of key literature. Using case studies, theories about normalisation are considered and applied to the daily activities of people with a learning disability. The impact of social stigma is considered, both in terms of self respect and of the value placed upon people with a learning disability by society at large.

Session objectives

When you have completed this session, you should be able to:

● define what is meant by the term 'normalisation'

● explain the origin of the concept and its early implications for institutional care

● evaluate normalisation as a principle for practice, and discuss its role in the move to community care for learning disability

● identify the impact of unconscious prejudice on the development of human services

● explain the concept of a conservative corollary to the principle of normalisation and assess its importance

● identify key accomplishments that services should try to achieve on behalf of users and apply this to an individual case study

● review the process of audit for the care environment in relation to the quality of care and the promotion of a 'normal' lifestyle.

1: Defining normalisation

The concept of **normalisation** has emerged as the basis for current approaches to learning disability services. To move towards defining the term in this context, it is useful to examine the structure of the word itself.

If we break the word down, the word 'normal' appears and, if we break it down further, the word 'norm' emerges. A 'norm' is a shared set of values which affect the actions of groups of individuals and promotes the emergence of similar patterns of behaviour and commonly held beliefs. We are not always conscious of these shared norms and values. The idea of individuality is very powerful in our society, so to think of each individual as being influenced in such a way to conform can be uncomfortable.

As the notion of adhering to the norm, or normative behaviour, is central to the development of an understanding of normalisation, we will take this a little further.

ACTIVITY 36   ALLOW 5 MINUTES

Consider the definition above of the word 'norm'. Then list below some situations in which you share with other people similar values and patterns of behaviour in your everyday life.

Commentary

There are many areas of everyday life that you could have chosen. Dress code is an area that I find useful to illustrate the idea of 'norms' in action. I have two main divisions in my dress code, namely casual and work clothes, but I can subdivide further. At home, I can dress for lounging, shopping, gardening or cleaning. Work clothes are more formal, but even here there are variations. Vital meetings may inspire a desire to 'power dress', for example. Certainly, when I attend a job interview, an important part of the process is choosing the right clothes, since it is through my physical presentation to others that I convey a specific message about myself. I am sure that you can identify occasions when you feel special dress to be necessary, and indeed 'normal' – for example, at weddings.

Subtle pressures exist which encourage our compliance with socially valued norms: these help the individual to fit in and feel part of the normal social arena. Whether we are 'normal' or not depends on the particular group or society to which we belong. What is accepted in one group is unacceptable in another. So the idea of normality as a constant needs to be challenged. A 'norm' is a theoretical concept which defines the attributes through which we attain normality.

A norm is less tangible than our feelings of normality; we can often *feel* the way we fit in but are not always conscious of why or how we do it. As social beings, we claim the right of individuality, of difference, but at the same time try to ensure that we remain acceptable to peers and powerful figures in our immediate society.

2: Key writers in the literature of normalisation

Emerson (1992) suggests there is no definitive concept of normalisation. Instead, he suggests there is 'a family of ideas that share a common ancestry'. Certainly, any review of the literature in this area indicates that definitions vary across cultures and times. You will probably also notice that the language used varies accordingly. We will take four key writers who have influenced the emergence of normalisation in this country, and examine the ways in which their ideas have developed over time. The four writers are Bank-Mikkelson, Nirje, Wolfensberger and O'Brien.

Bank-Mikkelson

The term normalisation first appeared in the Danish Mental Retardation Act of 1959, which was influenced by the work of Bank-Mikkelson (1980). For Bank-Mikkelson, normalisation meant [the creation of] 'an existence for the mentally retarded as close as possible to normal living conditions'. He later elaborated on this definition:

> '[Normalisation is]...making normal mentally retarded people's housing, education, working and leisure conditions. It means bringing them the legal and human rights of all other citizens.'

ACTIVITY 37   ALLOW **10** MINUTES

Note below what you think these definitions mean in practice, bearing in mind that they were first written in 1959.

Commentary

There is a clear intention here to benefit people with a learning disability. There is a recognition that for people who bear a negative image to be accepted in society, there must be some measure of acceptability in their lifestyle. Areas such as housing and education are mentioned. In other words, these people are seen to need help to 'fit in' with the society around them.

Bank-Mikkelson's definitions of normalisation provide a clear statement of intent, but the means to achieve this are not addressed in this early work.

Nirje

Ten years later, Nirje (1969), then executive director of the Swedish Association for Retarded Children, published the following definition of normalisation:

> *'Making available to mentally retarded people patterns of life and conditions as close as possible to the regular circumstances and ways of life of society.'*

Nirje outlined three handicaps: the actual learning disability of the individual; the imposed or acquired handicap; and the individual's personal awareness of their learning disability. There is not space to explore all of these, but the notion of secondary or acquired handicap is an important one to grasp.

ACTIVITY 38

ALLOW **10** MINUTES

This activity is presented in two sections.

1 Consider carefully what you think is meant by imposed or acquired handicap and write your ideas below, giving a few examples.

2 Consider the ways in which Nirje's definition of normalisation could diminish secondary handicaps. Add your ideas to your notes.

Commentary

Acquired handicap:
A handicap sustained as a consequence of trauma, usually in adulthood.

1 By an imposed or **acquired handicap** Nirje meant the additional limitations to development which occur as a consequence of negative modes of care. It is likely that you identified such additional handicaps as poor communication skills, being unable to carry out personal care such as bathing, going to the toilet, dressing and feeding oneself. These deficits in ability are described as imposed or additional because they are the consequence of the way in which vulnerable and stigmatised people have traditionally been cared for, rather than directly related to the initial learning disability. Nirje suggests that individual potential can be enhanced if an ordinary life pattern is made available.

2 Bank-Mikkelson had already addressed the issue of 'normal living conditions'. Nirje's definition implied a move away from traditional, dependent lifestyles and the adoption of a more independent, autonomous mode of living, albeit within an institutional framework, which would inhibit the development of secondary or acquired handicaps.

Another key phrase in Nirje's definition is 'patterns of life'. He used the term 'rhythms' later when he expanded on his definition. He referred to the rhythms of the day, the week, the year; to progression through the stages of the life cycle; and to self-determination and equal rights in work and living standards. The Nirje definition of normalisation aimed to restore rhythm and pattern to the life of the individual with learning disability.

Both Nirje's and Bank-Mikkelson's work in the area of normalisation was aimed at creating a better care environment, rather than promoting independent living. The improved conditions they referred to were improvements in the institutional approach to care. At the time, these influential figures saw no anomaly in proposing normalisation as an effective medium for improving existing care within a segregated environment. Emerson (1992) recorded three shared characteristics in the work of these two authors.

1 They are egalitarian statements about the rights of service users.

2 They focus on equality in terms of an individual's quality of life.

3 They do not specifically confront the issue of segregation in service design.

Wolfensberger

Wolfensberger, an American, was a highly influential figure in the development of normalisation as a principle for practice. Before Wolfensberger, normalisation had been proposed as a principle, without real consideration of the strategies which could be employed to make it a reality, and without threatening the status quo of the institution. Nirje and Bank-Mikkelson both put the principle of equality at the core of normalisation theory. However, the dilemma for many service providers who sought to establish normalisation in practice was the lack of *egalitarian practice* in relation to people with a learning disability.

Wolfensberger (1972) defined normalisation as the:

> '...utilization of means which are as culturally normative as possible, in order to establish and/or maintain personal behaviours and characteristics which are as culturally normative as possible.'

ACTIVITY 39   ALLOW **15** MINUTES

This definition is complex. Check your understanding of it by rewriting it in your own words, and then give an example of how it could be meaningful in practice.

Commentary

You may have started by clarifying the meaning of key words such as utilisation, means, and normative. *Utilisation* could be written as *use*; *means* could be written as *methods* or *ways*; while *normative* relates to norms, and could be considered to mean *usual*. *Culturally normative* could then become *acceptable*. This definition could be re-expressed as:

> 'Using methods which any person would find acceptable to help the individual to appear and behave in ways which other people would generally find acceptable.'

Your wording may be a bit different, but should convey something along these lines.

Wolfensberger's principal concern was the way in which people with a learning disability were forced to live in large institutions. A clear example of a 'normal' lifestyle would be to live in an ordinary house in an ordinary street. This would have a series of beneficial effects impacting upon the appearance and behaviour of an individual. Wider role models would be available and the influence of the local neighbourhood on behaviour would move individuals towards a shared ideal of approaches to living. Wolfensberger's concept of normalisation, applied in practice, could also include assisting individuals to dress and present themselves in such a way as to enable them to 'fit in' and enjoy an enhanced social worth. You may have thought of other examples but I hope this activity has helped you to grasp what Wolfensberger's rather obscurely worded definition means in practice.

ACTIVITY 40 — ALLOW 5 MINUTES

Identify the key difference between Wolfensberger's definition and those of the previous two Scandinavian writers.

Commentary

The key difference is, quite simply, that Wolfensberger provides both a defining statement and an indication that there are processes that can realise this intention.

Wolfensberger later re-defined normalisation as 'social role valorisation' (1983). He moved from describing the idea of normalisation to elaborating on the methods which should be used to create socially valued roles for disadvantaged groups.

ACTIVITY 41   ALLOW 10 MINUTES

Look up the word 'valorisation' in a dictionary. You may need to consider the word as a derivative of 'value'. Now, restate the phrase 'social role valorisation' in your own words.

Commentary

'Social role' refers to the roles or parts we play in society. For example, I play the role of mother, wife, teacher, writer, customer and friend, to name but a few. All of these roles have a value in our society. A part of the way in which I see myself is as a reflection of the value placed by others on the roles I play. If this value is positive and my roles are held in high esteem, then the value placed on me by society is also high, and my self-esteem is correspondingly enhanced. Conversely, if the roles I play are held in low esteem, then my perceived social value is low and it is also likely that my self-esteem will be low. To some extent, 'value' reflects the 'worth' that someone has. A restatement of **'social role valorisation'** could be, 'the process through which the worth of a person is measured by other members of society'.

Social role valorisation: *The creation of valued social roles for people with a learning disability.*

ACTIVITY 42   ALLOW 5 MINUTES

Place the following roles in a hierarchy, based on the esteem typically given to the holder of that role, starting with the highest.

doctor: nurse: teacher: postman/woman: clerical worker: secretary: shopkeeper: lawyer: dentist: road sweeper: lorry driver: taxi driver: checkout operator.

Commentary

My list places the professional groups at the top, starting with the doctor, dentist, lawyer, nurse and teacher. I would then place the remainder in some order beginning with secretary and ending with road sweeper. I realise that my list reflects some personal bias but if you think about social class for a moment you can see that these roles or jobs can be divided along class lines. My hierarchy represents the ways in which society rewards the holders of these roles, in terms of status, salary and working conditions. In our society, social esteem is given to the holders of professional roles. Manual jobs and unemployment do not attract the same esteem.

We shall now consider the way in which social values impact on the person with a learning disability. Wolfensberger's hierarchical structure of social role valorisation is reproduced in *Figure 4* below. The list can be read from the bottom up, the columns being actions which need to be taken to improve or enhance behaviour and self-presentation so that the ultimate goal, positive social valuation, can be achieved. This is a complex structure, but it is very useful in working out some of the approaches necessary to establish and/or maintain 'personal behaviours and characteristics which are as culturally normative as possible.'

The Hierarchical Structure of Social Role Valorization (Formerly Known as the Principle of Normalization)

The Ultimate Goal:
Enhancement of the Social Role of Persons or Groups at Risk of Social Devaluation, Via 2 Major Sub-Goals.

Enhancement of Their Social Image, via:				Enhancement of Their Personal Competencies, via:		
Physical Settings	Relationships and Groupings	Activities, Programmes, and Other Uses of Time	Language, and Other Symbols and Images	Physical Settings	Relationships and Groupings	Activities, Programmes & Other Uses of Time
Neighbourhood Harmony to Other Programmes	Enhancing Juxtaposition Workers	Enhancing Service Possessions	Enhancing Personal Families, Public	Accessibility to Clients, of Groupings	Enhancing Size and Composition of Needs	Address of Real and Urgent
Internal and External Appearance and and Features	Grouping Size that Facilitates Social Integration	Enhancing Separation of Programme Functions	Personal Appearance Integrative	Proximity to Potentially Resources	Enhancing Other Social Integration	Intense and Efficient Use
Enhancing Proximity to Other Sites	Enhancing Grouping Composition	Age and Culture Appropriate Activities and Schedules	Personal Labels and Service Names and Acronyms	Comfortable Environment	Programmatic Individualization	Provision/ Promotion of Enhancing Personal Possessions
Enhancing History	Enhancing Other Social Integration	Promotion of Autonomy and Rights	Enhancing Programme Funding	Challenging Environment	Life-Enriching Interactions	
				Individualiz- ation Facilit- ating Environment	Promotion of Valued Socio- Sexual Identity	

From Wolfensberger, W (1983) In: Mental Retardation Vol 21 No. 6 pp 234 – 239 American Association on Mental Deficiency.

Figure 4: Wolfensberger's hierarchical structure of social role valorisation

Take a few minutes to examine the hierarchical structure in *Figure 4*. Now take the middle column headed 'Language and other symbols and images' and study the list. Note down some comments on the relevance of the first item on this list, and then consider how this enhancement of personal possessions could be achieved.

Commentary

The low value or status given to people who have a learning disability is reinforced when their personal possessions are assessed. Many are on low incomes and have few possessions, which may be in disrepair or of poor quality. Visible poverty usually attracts a low social value. It is a sad reflection on our society that outward appearances can determine the behaviour of others towards us.

In practice, true ownership does not exist for many people with a learning disability. Living accommodation may be owned by others and ownership of furnishings collectively managed. The 'bag lady' is a potent image, but carrying one's possessions around is necessary for people whose living environment does not provide secure personal space. The person with a learning disability requires opportunities to develop self-respect that will lead to a valuing of their own personal possessions and hence to a valuing of the possessions of others and their right to safeguard them. Provision of a safe, secure living space is one aspect of a process that can help to enhance the social status of the individual with learning disability.

To enhance the personal possessions of people with a learning disability it is necessary to carry out an honest evaluation of their belongings. Within the normalisation literature frequent reference is made to the need for individuals to present themselves appropriately in relation to their age. This is often referred to as age-appropriate behaviour. Part of this age appropriateness is concerned with possessions. I have an enduring image of a woman in her late seventies whose constant companion was a teddy bear. The visible possession of this childish toy diminished her dignity in the eyes of others. All carers must realise the significance of possessions for making statements about who and what we are. This recognition must be taken into account when caring for someone, so that the rhythms of their life are reflected in their possessions.

Unconscious prejudice

Wolfensberger emphasises the need to adapt services in order to enable a positive social valuation of people with a learning disability to emerge. A review of the current system is an essential starting point for any process of change. However, Wolfensberger's work describes 'latent social intentions' which are rooted in unconscious prejudice. He argues that such prejudice has a highly negative impact on service development. It is therefore essential that these 'latent' or hidden prejudices are recognised if normalisation is to have a significant positive impact on individual lives. Powerful figures such as professional carers or teachers can prejudge an individual's ability to the extent that restricted experiences and opportunities occur as a matter of course. This may in turn reinforce stigma.

ACTIVITY 44

ALLOW **10** MINUTES

Think back to the work you completed on prejudice in Sessions One and Two. Can you think of some examples of unconscious prejudice within a service (not just health or social care services) towards particular social groups? Give at least two examples of such prejudice in action.

Commentary

British society maintains many social prejudices in relation to race, gender and age, as well as disability. Prejudices concerning race or gender are often unconscious rather than blatant. One example of unconscious prejudice is found in the number of black male children who are referred to special education services, despite the fact that they have measured IQs within normal parameters. You can find out more about this from Sally Tomlinson's work on the sociology of special education (1982).

The conservatism corollary

Wolfensberger argued that a devalued social role is a corollary or consequence of multiple devaluing characteristics possessed by an individual or group.

ACTIVITY 45

ALLOW **10** MINUTES

List some of the 'multiple devaluing characteristics' of people with a learning disability that have been mentioned so far.

Commentary

It is likely that you have listed some of these characteristics, although your wording may differ from mine: the visible condition itself; poverty of dress and self-presentation; limited intellectual functioning; the absence of standard speech patterns; and the presence of associated medical conditions which are themselves a source of stigmatisation, such as epilepsy and Down's syndrome.

Wolfensberger and Thomas (1983) suggested that an overcompensation towards conservative, or average, norms should become an essential part of the positive revaluing process. In other words, to undo centuries of poor public image, this group of stigmatised people should present themselves in as conforming a manner as possible. This is the 'conservatism corollary' to the principle of normalisation.

Conservatism corollary: *Wolfensberger's theory that the greater the visible difference from the 'norm' a person appears to be, the greater is the need for that individual to present to society a 'conformist' or 'conservative' appearance.*

ACTIVITY 46	ALLOW 5 MINUTES

Suggest at least two positive outcomes which might arise from the conservatism corollary concept.

Commentary

A wide range of positive outcomes are possible. For example, if the average or normative mode of dress became the norm for people in care, they would cease to be identifiable by the apparent absence of fashion sense. (This is *not* the same thing as dressing uniformly, and the uniformity that results from the bulk buying of clothing should be avoided by carers.) In the same way, the adoption of normative rules or codes of behaviour in their social interactions with others would improve the public image of people with learning disability.

This compensatory mechanism means that potentially stigmatised people become less noticeable and the negative social impact of difference is reduced.

ACTIVITY 47	ALLOW 5 MINUTES

Suggest at least two possible negative outcomes which might arise from the conservatism corollary idea.

Commentary

One outcome is that the conservatism itself can become so uniform as to create a new negative image, a sort of 'grey' person. Another is that, by reinforcing the average, the unexpected could then start to create confusion. The absence of spontaneity could reinforce prejudicial attitudes towards the intellectually disabled. The question also arises as to whose sense of the conservative is to be adopted. Powerful carers are in a position to impose restrictions based on their own preferences.

When I think about the 'conservatism corollary', I am reminded of two incidents in my experience as a carer. Within one particular hospital, the management had become converted to the principle of normalisation and decreed that this philosophy should permeate all aspects of the care environment. This led to a requirement that the dress code for all those in care in this hospital should be of a formal and conservative style. The outcome was that the individuality of each person became submerged as much by this well-intentioned directive as by past lack of care.

The second incident happened as I walked to work one morning. I was aware of someone coming towards me from the opposite end of the street. Something had caught my attention. The person moving towards me was carrying a very brightly painted snooker cue case. As he came closer, I saw that he was physically disabled and had an extreme gait. My immediate thought was 'Imagine letting someone whose disability is so visible carry something like a case that just draws attention to him'. No sooner did the thought occur than I realised that I had noticed the case before the disability. In this case, the absence of conservatism acted to reduce stigma.

Wolfensberger's work took the idea of normalisation and placed it within an historical and social context that could be acted upon to improve services for people with a learning disability. We will now move on to our final author, John O'Brien.

O'Brien

Like Wolfensberger, O'Brien's concern has been with the ways normalisation can have an impact on care services. With Tyne, he is the most prominent of the British writers on normalisation. Emerson (1992) says:

> 'O'Brien's interpretation of normalisation can be seen to represent a return to the values underpinning the initial conceptions of normalisation and a retreat from the grand theorising of Wolfensberger.'

O'Brien's central concern is to outline or delineate the key issues that services should accomplish for users. This has resulted in the emergence of the 'five accomplishments', which we will consider in turn. These accomplishments are:

- community presence
- making choices
- enabling competence
- enhancing respect
- community participation.

Community presence

This refers to the need to ensure that service users are present in the community and that they have access to the same facilities as everyone else. The need for an integrated lifestyle is emphasised.

ACTIVITY 48 — ALLOW 5 MINUTES

Can you think of ways in which service users could live in a community but have little community presence?

Commentary

It would be possible to establish a community home within a small village, for example, but neglect to establish some involvement with the core community. Presence is established through using local services such as the GP, shops, clubs or church. If central supplies are used or an insular lifestyle develops, then integration becomes limited to mere physical presence rather than a genuine community presence.

Making choices

Service users need to be supported in making choices about their lifestyle. To achieve this, individuals need help to understand their situation, the range of options open to them, and practice in making decisions of a personal nature at all stages of their life.

ACTIVITY 49 — ALLOW 3 MINUTES

Think back to the first hour of waking today. How many decisions did you make in that first hour?

Commentary

You may initially have answered 'none', because we tend to think of choice in terms of major decisions and fail to realise how many minor areas of choice exist in our lives. For example, our time of rising, order of dressing, washing and eating, all involve an element of choice, albeit within certain constraints. As we grow up we find ourselves with a greater range of choices, but at each stage we are aware of the parameters which determine the nature of our decision-making. If people do not have control over the small decisions, it is unlikely that they will be equipped to handle major life decisions.

Enabling competence

We have already discussed the need for devalued groups to be given opportunities to develop skills and attributes which are valued in their community. Competence in this context means that individuals are empowered to become competent within areas that are usual for all. The consequence of this should be that dependence is significantly decreased and that personal characteristics are positively developed.

Enhancing respect

Powerful groups do not have respect for people with a learning disability, as they lack the presentation of self which promotes value and respect. Moreover, the stigmatised individual often lacks self-respect, seeing him or herself through the eyes of others. The combination of these two factors can lead to a self-fulfilling prophecy, a vicious circle, wherein self-worth is permanently inhibited.

ACTIVITY 50　　　　ALLOW 10 MINUTES

Consider the two issues of respect and competence for a moment. In what ways do they interact? How can you promote their development?

Commentary

Respect and competence are intertwined in what is almost a 'chicken and egg' situation. Without competence there is little respect from others, and in the absence of this respect it is difficult to encourage the development of competence. The practitioner in this area must begin by reinforcing the individual's self-respect. From self-respect grows, at the very least, an absence of disrespect by others, and also an enhanced appreciation of one's own potential. This stage is a precursor to the development of competence, an attribute that engages the full respect of others.

Community participation

Presence in the community has degrees of impact. If the presence is real and complemented by developments in competence and respect, then positive participation in the community can be promoted. Participation in the community should reflect individual needs and preferences, providing opportunities for the widening of networks.

ACTIVITY 51 ALLOW **15** MINUTES

Case study

> Jack, Maureen, Anna and Marick share a house on a large housing association estate. They are all able to get about and have a range of self-caring skills. Jack and Anna can articulate well and are understood by strangers. Both had part-time jobs cleaning in a pub, but the move to this house meant that they could not continue in their jobs. Maureen has some hip problems but manages well, although experiencing some pain in cold weather. Marick is shy, although he likes his house companions. Together, they keep house and look after themselves, although they appreciate the weekly visit of the support worker from the community team for learning disabilities.

Using *Figure 5* below, plot strategies that will enhance the five accomplishments for the members of this home.

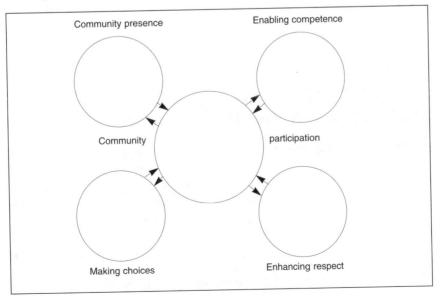

Figure 5: Action plan to implement the five accomplishments

Commentary

There are a range of suitable alternatives to the ideas suggested here. Compare your suggestions with mine, in *Figure 6* below.

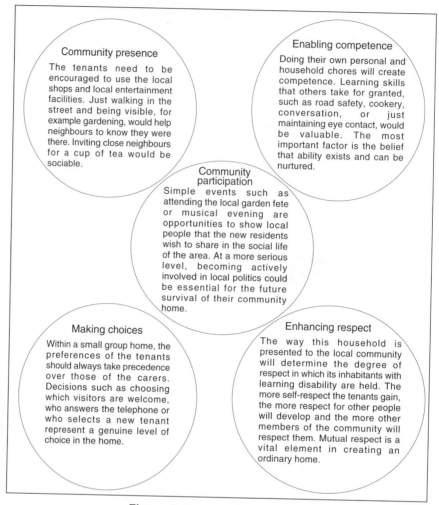

Community presence

The tenants need to be encouraged to use the local shops and local entertainment facilities. Just walking in the street and being visible, for example gardening, would help neighbours to know they were there. Inviting close neighbours for a cup of tea would be sociable.

Enabling competence

Doing their own personal and household chores will create competence. Learning skills that others take for granted, such as road safety, cookery, conversation, or just maintaining eye contact, would be valuable. The most important factor is the belief that ability exists and can be nurtured.

Community participation

Simple events such as attending the local garden fete or musical evening are opportunities to show local people that the new residents wish to share in the social life of the area. At a more serious level, becoming actively involved in local politics could be essential for the future survival of their community home.

Making choices

Within a small group home, the preferences of the tenants should always take precedence over those of the carers. Decisions such as choosing which visitors are welcome, who answers the telephone or who selects a new tenant represent a genuine level of choice in the home.

Enhancing respect

The way this household is presented to the local community will determine the degree of respect in which its inhabitants with learning disability are held. The more self-respect the tenants gain, the more respect for other people will develop and the more other members of the community will respect them. Mutual respect is a vital element in creating an ordinary home.

Figure 6: Suggested action plan

We have moved from exploring the theory of normalisation to some consideration of the impact of this theory on service provision. We are now going to focus on the ways in which normalisation can help to improve the quality of life of people with a learning disability.

3: Quality audit – measuring the impact of normalisation theory on practice

Normalisation has been used as a guide in the development of audit tools that measure the effectiveness of a service. The terms 'quality' and 'audit' often seem threatening when applied to service delivery. However, at the heart of the process of empowering people with a learning disability is the imperative to listen to them, act on their statements and promote their ability to speak for themselves. We are going to introduce two key books specially written to help the service provider review service provision through the experiences of the service user.

Evaluation of service provision by the service user – three methods

In *Service Evaluation by People with Learning Difficulties* Whittaker (1991) writes 'The document is intended to be used as a tool in assessing the quality of service being received by users of residential services for adults with a learning difficulty.' The document is based on the work of Wolfensberger, O'Brien, and the King's Fund report (1980).

ACTIVITY 52 — ALLOW 25 MINUTES

Resource 10 in the *Resources Section* contains an overview of the lifestyle dimensions covered in the document. Read it and consider to what extent the principles of normalisation are reflected in the intentions outlined for EQUAL – IF.

Commentary

Nirje's rhythms of life and Wolfensberger's ideas of empowerment and an ordinary life are reflected in the intentions of this package. O'Brien's five accomplishments are also clearly visible.

Central to the document's evaluation of quality of life is a detailed assessment of lifestyle. The format for this assessment is a lengthy questionnaire which is applied both to the user of the service and to the member of staff responsible for that individual's care. The problem with this is that the carer can retain control of this process and perhaps even decide that the individual concerned is not able to make any comment on these areas of life. Such a decision, of course, overturns the principle guiding the document. This thought reminds us that at the core of normalisation is the principle of establishing the right to an ordinary life for people with a learning disability. This includes the right to report on whether their experiences are good or bad.

A second report, by Whittaker et al. (1991) moves normalisation truly into the realms of practice. It is very different from the EQUAL – IF report. Although the focus for both reports is the person with a learning disability, EQUAL – IF placed the expertise in the realm of the service provider. The Whittaker report focuses firmly on the individual service user. The unusual element in Whittaker's book is that the people who use the services also carried out the research.

ACTIVITY 53

'The evaluation was really very simple. So why cannot we adopt this approach universally? It just needs a bit of courage to be prepared to listen to the real experts, people who experience our service every day. Service users do not feel free to comment honestly to the staff who provide the services.'

Think about the above quote from the Whittaker report for a moment and then identify some reasons why people may feel that they cannot say what they truly think about the quality of the services they receive.

Commentary

The rest of the quotation provides one possible answer. 'The users are dependent on the service and may fear what will happen to them if they are too outspoken.' There are also tensions in relationships between staff and clients. Staff may feel they are doing their best to provide good care, but the clients may feel disempowered by the process of care. No-one likes to hurt another's feelings when they are aware that the offending actions are well-intentioned.

Whittaker et al. (1991) outline their strategy in this book and I recommend it to you as a useful guide in this area. Let us now consider briefly how you can use the knowledge gained in this session to look at how far the services *you* provide adhere to the principles of normalisation.

ACTIVITY 54

Consider ways in which you could find out how people who have limited facility with language could indicate their degree of satisfaction with services. Try to produce some ideas for the development of a potential scale of satisfaction.

Commentary

My first thought was to review some of the methods developed to help non-speaking children to indicate the degree of pain they experience. The most effective way seemed to me to be the use of faces with a range of smiles and frowns to indicate degree. This method has been used by Whittaker et al. (1991) to good effect.

Many variations on this theme are possible. I thought about a range of roman candle type fireworks, no fizz being low and multi-coloured sparkles being high. It should be possible to develop a range of tools to cover the different aspects of life that are relevant to different individuals. The important thing is for the user to be aware that his or her opinions matter and will be taken seriously.

Summary

1   We have explored the concept of normalisation and applied the principles to learning disability.

2   We have discussed the importance given to social role and to social role valorisation.

3   We have discovered how people with a learning disability can attract a devaluing label.

4   We have explored the means by which people with a learning disability can develop a positive presence in the community and achieve a normal lifestyle.

Before you move on to Session Four, check that you have achieved the objectives given at the beginning of this session and, if not, review the appropriate section.

SESSION FOUR

Teaching skills

Introduction

Your work with people with a learning disability will inevitably involve you in a teaching role. The aim of this session is to enable you to explore this role. Effective teaching is made up of many skills. This session provides opportunities to identify and develop ways of using these teaching skills with clients and informal carers. You are not expected to undertake the same level of work as a qualified and experienced teacher. Because it is a practical session, there are more activities than in some of the other sessions, but they are also shorter.

Session objectives

When you have completed this session you should be able to:

- evaluate the processes of teaching and learning

- plan, implement and evaluate a teaching session

- develop a teaching programme for clients in a chosen area of interest

- understand and use structured teaching strategies in creating a learning opportunity

- develop skills in creating learning programmes for people with limited literacy skills

- assist informal carers in developing their own teaching skills.

For this session you will need to identify a client that you wish to work with. This client will be the focus for some of the activities.

1: Your role as teacher

Teaching will probably be a significant part of your role in working with people with a learning disability. Your teaching may take many forms. Let's start by thinking about *who* you teach.

ACTIVITY 55 ALLOW 5 MINUTES

1 Think back over your last few shifts, and reflect on the nature of your involvement with the people you came into contact with.

2 List five of the people that you came into contact with below.

   1

   2

   3

   4

   5

3 Put a tick next to those people on the list where your contact involved any form of teaching.

Commentary

You are likely to have come into contact with clients, informal carers (relatives or friends), colleagues, peers and other professionals, to mention just a few. If you have not made many ticks, have another think. Could some of the activities that you are involved in be considered teaching but you have not really thought of them as such?

Don't limit yourself to thinking of a classroom situation.

ACTIVITY 56 ALLOW 5 MINUTES

Take a few minutes to think about the different ways we can be taught something. List them below.

Commentary

Teaching can involve a number of activities. It can include amongst others giving a demonstration, giving instructions or information, and encouraging trial and error or experimentation, for example.

ACTIVITY 57
ALLOW 3 MINUTES

Look back at Activity 56. Did your contact with people in the last few days involve any of the above activities? If so, please say what they were.

Commentary

You might have mentioned things like helping someone to learn how to dress or cross the road. Perhaps you had to show a new colleague how to use a lifting aid or maybe you were asked by a relative to explain the implications of a new drug that has been prescribed.

These examples illustrate how you become involved in teaching as part of your daily work. You may not have thought of some of these activities as teaching before, but it is something that can occur in many ways in a range of settings.

ACTIVITY 58
ALLOW 2 MINUTES

French (1983) lists 15 possible ways in which teaching can occur. Look through the list below. Put a circle round those forms of teaching that you use often, underline the ones you use occasionally, and put a cross against the ones you never use.

explanation	demonstration
lecture	modelling
talk	project work
free group discussion	simulated experience
directed group discussion	seminar
workshop	reading
observation	participant observation
counselling	

Commentary

It may be that some of the types of teaching which you don't use are inappropriate for your work setting, for example, lectures. Others may not be used because you do not feel confident about working in this way. All of the approaches listed have advantages for the learner and teacher. Some approaches are more appropriate for some types of learning.

We can be influenced in our choice of teaching methods by our experience of learning situations.

ACTIVITY 59   ALLOW **10** MINUTES

Think of teaching methods that you have experienced as a learner. Under each heading write down an occasion when you learnt:

Something practical (a new skill)

Emotional (an insight about yourself)

Social (a new way of behaving)

Intellectual (a new piece of knowledge)

For each example, make brief notes in the remaining space on each of the questions below:

1   What was the method used by the teacher?

2   Was it appropriate for you?

3   Did you find it easy to learn this way?

4   Would you have preferred to be taught another way?

Commentary

This activity may have helped you to appreciate that some teaching methods are much better suited to particular situations than others. For example, it is unlikely that you were taught to give an injection by lecture. It is far more effective to give a practical demonstration, after which you can be supervised and guided through it.

Some teaching methods are of particular value when working with people with a learning disability.

ACTIVITY 60 — ALLOW 5 MINUTES

List any teaching methods that you have used or can recall being used with people with a learning disability.

Commentary

Probably the most commonly used methods are:

- **task analysis**, where the learning is broken down into easily managed steps

- **modelling**, where the teacher demonstrates an activity which the student then imitates

- **play**, which can be used with adults as well as children. Role play is a form of imaginative play and is useful in practising a range of social skills. Creative play, using drama or art therapy for example, can aid the development of a range of skills including communication.

Did you also note down incidental teaching – those unplanned opportunities that arise out of other activities like going to the shops or cinema? Daily life provides opportunities for many learning experiences.

2: Factors that influence the teaching/ learning process

ACTIVITY 61 — ALLOW 10 MINUTES

1 Think of a time when you successfully learned something. What factors can you identify that helped you learn?

2 Identify a time when you had difficulty learning. What factors contributed to the problems?

Commentary

A central theme in the learning process is motivation. A student who is not motivated to learn is unlikely to achieve the identified learning outcomes. Maslow (1968) suggested that people are motivated by physical, psychological and social factors. Often it is the external or extrinsic rewards that we gain from completing a piece of learning that provide the motivation to carry on. The reward might be monetary (for example, a pay rise on completing a course of study) or simply convenience (for example, time saved on learning how to use a computer). The regard that others have for us can also be a driving force. Knowing that our parents or partners will be proud of our achievements can be an important influence. Motivation also consists of intrinsic factors – those feelings of self-esteem that come from achieving something.

Other factors may also have helped you to learn, such as receiving positive feedback and being given encouragement by the teacher for your efforts. You may also have mentioned feeling comfortable, being at ease or feeling safe, or feeling that your presence was valued.

The social and emotional environment is very important in learning situations. You will probably have recalled feelings of discomfort that contributed to difficult learning situations. Emotional factors can be barriers to learning, for example:

● if we are made to feel stupid or foolish when we do not understand or make a mistake

● if we are not sure about what is expected and are afraid to ask

● if we are not given adequate guidance and support

● if we feel that we are not accepted in the group.

Physical factors can hinder our ability to learn, too. Have you ever tried to concentrate when you are tired or hungry, or got lost in a lecture because you forgot your glasses and could not see the overhead projector screen?

We all respond differently to learning situations and our needs are equally individual.

People with a learning disability will respond to learning in a similar way to the rest of us but may have a greater number of learning needs. These have to be considered together with any special needs and the possibility of negative and even distressing experiences of learning in the past.

ACTIVITY 62

Bearing in mind what we have said about establishing a positive learning environment, write a checklist of questions to consider when setting up a learning situation with a group of people with a learning disability. It may be helpful to make notes under the headings below.

Physical

Social

Emotional

Commentary

Your list may differ in some places from mine, but these are the key questions that you need to address.

Physical | Is the location warm, comfortable, considerate of physical disabilities?

Are the individual members of the group comfortable? Are they hungry or tired? Has account been taken of special needs – hearing, sight? Are comfortable chairs provided?

Social | Is the group a suitable mix, does it encourage interaction?

Is the group size appropriate?

Is there recognition of the individuals in the group?

Emotional | Have you praised effort?

Have you caused ridicule?

Have you accepted mistakes?

Did you explain expectations?

Were you consistent?

Did you encourage supportive behaviour within the group?

Did you listen?

3: Assessing learning needs

ACTIVITY 63 ALLOW 10 MINUTES

Think of two or three people whom you have recently taught. (These could be people you identified in the first activities of this session.) Note down what you taught them and why that particular learning activity was chosen.

Who was taught   What they were taught   Why the activity was taught

Commentary

I cannot guess the reasons you have given, but I have listed some common ones below. Check how they compare with yours.

1   Someone has just been on a course and is eager to try out their new skills and pass on new knowledge.

2   The activity was the next one in a skill development programme.

3   The activity was identified as necessary for a particular situation, for example, the person needed to be able to cross the road in order to go shopping.

4   Assessment had identified that a need could be met by mastering that particular activity.

ACTIVITY 64 ALLOW 5 MINUTES

Do some of these reasons make more sense than others? Make notes on the possible strengths and weaknesses of each rationale.

1

2

3

4

Commentary

1 Whilst it is important that people get the opportunity to use new skills, they need to be applied appropriately. If a new skill fits in with the programme of care, all well and good, but if not, then it can lead to inconsistency within the care plan. If new skills are irrelevant to the person's needs, there is no clear rationale for including them. In this situation, it may be more useful to consider the adaptability of the principles underlying the teacher's newly acquired skills.

2 Structured teaching systems have a rigid development theme, and the weaknesses discussed above may also apply here. If programmes are not tailored to meet the individual's needs, time can be wasted on learning that is not particularly relevant to the learner.

3 A lack of skills needed for one activity can lead to the loss of other opportunities. It is suggested, for example, that if a person cannot cross the road, they cannot go shopping either. Teaching someone to cross the road may be the logical next step, but this is not necessarily so. If we think about the skills involved in going shopping and crossing the road, they are very different. Should a lack of ability in one area preclude a person from the opportunity to experience another? It may be more appropriate to assist someone to cross the road, while they master the skills involved in shopping, and then to reassess the situation. If going to the shop involves crossing a busy main road and the person does not walk quickly, it may not be realistic or logical to achieve this, or it may be a long-term project. Persisting may simply make the person demoralised and resistant to new teaching situations.

4 The value of this approach depends on the quality of the assessment, but a proper assessment of need ensures that there is knowledge of what a person can already do. This can be used as a framework to build upon, facilitating individual and consistent approaches to meeting the person's needs.

ACTIVITY 65　　　　　　ALLOW 15 MINUTES

Case study

> **Harry** lives with his elderly mother who until recently was very active. A month ago she had a mild stroke and is now unable to help Harry with his daily living needs as she spends much of her day confined to bed.
>
> Harry goes to a day centre and is collected by bus at 8.30 a.m. each weekday. Until her stroke, his mother used to wake him up, prepare his breakfast, help him dress and wash and see him to the bus outside the front gate.
>
> If Harry was to remain at home he needed to be able to perform this early morning routine with the minimum of supervision from his mother.
>
> A worker was placed to assist Harry in his training for the early morning routine. This seemed fairly straightforward to the care worker. She identified a range of skills that Harry would need:
>
> ● telling the time, for getting up and leaving the house

- dressing appropriately

- personal care such as washing and hair care

- preparing food for breakfast.

The worker tried to teach Harry to tell the time. The first problem was that he had no numeracy skills: he did not know numbers. He also had great problems deciding what to wear. Even when his clothes were chosen he looked very dishevelled when he dressed himself. He had a lot of trouble with his buttons. Four months later, both Harry and the care worker were very disillusioned. Harry was no nearer to telling the time or dressing himself independently and the care worker had exchanged her role of teacher for that of 'doer'. She now arrived in time to get Harry up, dressed and washed him, gave him breakfast and saw him out of the house.

Can you identify some of the reasons why the training programme had been so unsuccessful?

Commentary

You probably realised that the scope of the training had been too broad. A range of skills had been introduced but Harry had mastered none. He did not have the prerequisite skills for some of the training activities chosen and, not surprisingly, Harry and the care worker gave up. Both lost their motivation in the light of constant failure.

ACTIVITY 66   ALLOW 5 MINUTES

Can you think of any broad principles which might have been usefully applied at the start of this programme?

Commentary

The case study shows that a training programme must start from the individual's starting point, and must identify outcomes that are achievable. The use of a comprehensive assessment to highlight the individual's ability or dependency level will give a guide to what could be included as a learning activity.

Numerous checklists are commercially available that can be used as aids to the assessment process. However a checklist can only tell you what a person can and cannot do. It does not necessarily identify *why* a person cannot do something. We shall return to this shortly.

Once needs have been accurately identified, it is easier to identify relevant and achievable outcomes. In Harry's case, the desired outcomes were set too high and were too complex. Do you have to be able to tell the time to get up at the correct time? Could the use of an alarm clock be sufficient to create a much more realistic goal?

Perhaps aiming to teach Harry how to set an alarm clock would have been much more successful and certainly less stressful for everyone. The success would probably have motivated him to willingly take on the next activity. As MacNamara (1995) states, too often random skills are taught and not retained because they were not needed or wanted by the trainee in the first place.

Does Harry have clothes that are easier for him to put on? Success with simple fastenings at first would perhaps motivate him to tackle buttons later. On the other hand, if he is unlikely to manage buttons by himself at all, it is counter productive to ask him to struggle with them.

Let's consider the importance of identifying all the information about someone's ability in a particular activity, including the reasons why they cannot do something.

ACTIVITY 67 ALLOW 5 MINUTES

Take an example of a daily activity: fastening shoe laces. List all the possible reasons why a person may not be able to fasten their shoe laces.

Commentary

There are a number of possible reasons. You may have noted something along these lines:

- physical disability: the person has poor fine motor control

- lack of opportunity: the person has always had Velcro fastenings before

- lack of incentive: the person knows that someone else will fasten the laces

- lack of teaching: this skill has has not been taught.

An understanding of the underlying cause of the deficit should influence exactly what skill is taught and how it is taught. It is necessary to consider both the learning ability and the learning needs of the person concerned, as this will influence the teaching method to be used.

4: Planning your teaching

Having identified what a person's learning needs are, it is very important that the teaching is thoroughly planned. Mager (1972) says 'If you are not certain of where you are going you may well end up somewhere else and not even know it'. People with a learning disability can find it difficult to make progress in learning new skills and often need highly structured help. This needs very careful planning.

Effective planning, whilst time-consuming, can save much wasted time later. Like the house built on shaky foundations, poorly planned teaching will crumble. We are going to focus on two aspects of planning: establishing goals and choosing teaching methods. We shall specifically discuss one-to-one teaching and it would be helpful for you to have a familiar client in mind as you work through the following pages.

We saw earlier that incentive is a strong motivator to learn and that, if motivation is lacking, the chances of success are slim. It is important, therefore, that the client is involved throughout the teaching process and that the planning stage should involve them in selecting goals.

Establishing goals

Learning needs have to be translated into goals or outcomes. Long-term goals can be too remote, so it is useful to break them down into a series of short-term goals which lead towards the long-term desired outcome.

Identifying goals is an important feature of the teaching process and should be communicated precisely for all to see. It is the first step towards producing a plan of action. MacNamara (1995) proposes that a clear goal statement should show:

- who   trainee

- will do what   the task

- under what conditions   the circumstances

- to what level of success   the criteria

- with what result   the motivator

- in what length of time   time plan

ACTIVITY 68

1 In the space below, identify a long-term goal for a client that you are working with. I have given you two examples to illustrate what I mean by a long-term goal.

Example 1 Jenny will do the shopping at the local supermarket.

Example 2 George will eat using a spoon.

2 Now identify a short-term goal that will help you move towards the long-term outcome. Again, I have given you two examples which I hope will give you enough information to develop your own.

Example 1 Jenny will name a range of basic food items from the shelves in the supermarket. To include bread, meat, fruit, vegetables, margarine, milk, coffee, soap.

Example 2 George will hold a spoon.

The teaching of new skills to people with a learning disability can take some time. Many long-term goals will have to be broken down into a series of small steps which will take the person from their current level of skill to the achieving of the long-term goal. This breaking down of skills into very small stages is called **task analysis**.

Task analysis: *The breakdown of stages of learning that assist in creating the process of error-free learning.*

ACTIVITY 69

1 Think about what is involved in an activity such as putting on a coat. Write down all the stages involved in completing this task. When you have done this, look at my task analysis below and note any differences.

2 Now do a task analysis of the short-term goal you chose in the last activity. If possible, ask someone else to analyse this task and then compare your results with theirs.

1 Putting on a coat

2   Your own short-term goal

Commentary

I would suggest that a breakdown of putting on a coat should look something like this:

- pick up the coat by the collar

- turn the jacket so the sleeves are in the right position

- hold the lapel with the left hand

- put right arm through the right sleeve and push

- let go with the left hand

- put your left arm behind your back

- find the armhole

- put your left arm into armhole and push

- hunch the jacket up onto shoulders

- pull the front together by positioning each lapel.

I cannot know what short-term goal you chose, but if you compare your two attempts at task analysis with other people's, you may well find that we all have quite different ways of approaching the same task. Someone who is left-handed, for example, might need to approach some tasks the other way round to a right-handed person. This illustrates how important it is to be precise when you plan to teach a skill, if confusion for the learner is to be avoided. It also reinforces the need for clear written communication via a teaching plan for all those involved.

Teaching methods

In an earlier activity you considered a list of teaching methods. The appropriate method will depend on what is to be taught, and on what suits the individual learner. Several strategies are particularly useful when using a highly structured approach in one-to-one teaching situations. Three commonly used methods are chaining, prompting and reinforcement.

Chaining

Forward chaining: A process of error-free learning that commences at the starting point of the learning chain and builds up in small stages of each part of the task step by step, until the total learning is achieved.

Backward chaining: A process of error-free learning that begins at the end point of the learning chain and builds up in small stages each part of the task, step by step, until the total learning is achieved

In **forward chaining** the learner masters one step of the task analysis at a time, in the order that the task would be carried out. In **backward chaining** the learner masters each step in the reverse order that it would be carried out. For example, if putting on a coat, the teacher completes most of the task but leaves the last step – straightening up the lapels – for the learner to complete. When this is mastered, the last two steps – straightening the lapels and hunching the jacket onto the shoulders – are left for the learner to complete. This is a useful method because the learner sees the whole task through and has the satisfaction of finishing the task with something they can do.

Prompting

Prompting consists of physical prompts, as in holding the learner's hand over a spoon if learning to feed; gestural prompts, as in pointing or miming an action; and verbal prompts, as in giving a word or phrase to prompt the learner. If using prompting, it is necessary gradually to fade out the prompts. The aim is for the task to be completed independently, so that as the learner becomes more proficient, the teacher reduces the prompts. Fading should be used carefully, not be introduced too soon and not be too prolonged.

Prompting:
Something which strengthens a learned response.

Reinforcement

Reinforcement is a recognised strategy to support the learning of new skills. It is the action that lets the learner know that a desired behaviour has occurred. Reinforcement strengthens new behaviour. Primary reinforcers are those that are essential to life like food and drink. Secondary reinforcers are those that are not of value in themselves but can be exchanged for other things. Examples would be money, tokens or stars. Social reinforcement consists of encouragements such as smiles, praise or hugs.

Reinforcement:
Rewarding behaviour– making it more likely to happen again.

In theory it may seem that prompting and reinforcement are simple, straightforward concepts. However, in practice this is not always so. Consider the next activity.

ACTIVITY 70   ALLOW **10** MINUTES

Think back to your client and the task analysis that you did earlier. What methods would be appropriate for teaching the tasks you analysed?

Commentary

If you chose a goal such as putting on a coat which involves a series of physical manipulations, backward chaining would be an appropriate method to choose. This provides a very structured method of teaching and is particularly helpful when relatives or carers are to be involved. Breaking the activity down into precise stages minimises the risk of confusion or error. In many care environments a number of people will be involved with the learner and it is important that everybody approaches the teaching activity in the same manner. This requires careful planning and co-ordinated teamwork.

5: Writing a teaching plan

A teaching plan is a written document that clearly records the key information about the student and what you are intending to teach. It should include:

- relevant biographical details

- assessment of learning need and ability

- the objectives or goals identified

- the teaching methods or strategies to be used

- a section to allow evaluation of the learning achieved.

ACTIVITY 71   ALLOW **10** MINUTES

What are the benefits of producing a teaching plan? List your ideas below.

Commentary

The main benefits of writing a teaching plan include the written record of the explicit nature of the student and teacher activity. This should enhance the level of consistency in approach and is particularly valuable if several people are to be involved, or when the teaching is mainly done by a relative or carer. In stating clearly and concisely exactly what the carer has to do, the plan enables effective monitoring and evaluation of the teaching activities. A teaching plan is not just an aid to planning teaching then; it is also a valuable tool to facilitate the communication that is essential if all those involved are to achieve consistency and co-ordination of teaching activities.

Figure 7 sets out details of the kind of background information that is needed before you can develop a teaching plan.

Name of student	
Address/place of residence	
Age	
Sex	
Cultural background	
Carer names	
Primary language of	
Student	
Carer	
Notes on previous learning experience	

Figure 7: Teaching plan – general background information

Assessment	Goals or Objectives	Planning	Implementation	Evaluation
Assessment of the ability/ achievement	Long-term goals broken down into realistic short-term goals	When to start the programme	Breakdown of activity with precise details as to what teacher must do	Have the goals been met?
Barriers to learning, i.e. physical, behavioural, social and cultural	Expressed in terms of what the student will be able to do	Teaching methods to be used		Yes – set new goals or move on to already established goals
		Outline of the sequence of learning steps (e.g. a task analysis)		No – review each stage of the process
Parental ability, availability and willingness to be involved		Reinforcement to be used. Who is to be involved. Nature of record keeping		

Figure 8: Developing a teaching plan

ACTIVITY 72 ALLOW **20** MINUTES

Using the stages in *Figure 8*, work out a teaching plan for one of the following situations.

Case Study 1

> **David** is a nine-year-old boy who has Down's syndrome. He lives at home with his parents and two younger brothers. David does very little self-caring activities for himself and his mother finds it easier and quicker to do things for him. You agree with David's mother that it would be beneficial to both David and her if David began to do more for himself. You agree to establish a programme aimed towards teaching David to put on his coat.

Case Study 2

> **Angela** is a 25-year-old woman who has a learning disability. She lives in a group home with three other women. Four days a week she works in the kitchen of a local café. She is very overweight and gets breathless if she exerts herself. Angela appreciates that she is overweight and would like to lose weight but it is obvious that she has little understanding of nutritional values.

Commentary

Case Study 1

Your plan will probably look similar to the one in *Figure 9*. Note that this plan makes use of the kind of task analysis that was discussed earlier. *Figure 10* shows how the precise details of David's progress can be recorded simply and clearly.

Case Study 2

Angela's plan (*Figure 11*) illustrates the particular needs of people with few or no iteracy skills. Although there is a lot of health education material available, much of it requires a relatively high level of literacy. When teaching people with a learning disability it is often necessary to create teaching tools that are appropriate to their ability and understanding. The use of visual material is very valuable for people with poor literacy skills as complex concepts can be understood more easily through pictures. A range of visual material such as cartoons, photographs and comic book stories can be used to help get messages over. Doak et al. (1996) have written extensively about teaching people with low literacy skills and it may be helpful to consult their work.

Evaluation

Evaluation of your teaching and of the student's learning is an important quality check. It enables you to assess the success of your teaching and to make changes if progress is not what you had hoped for. Progress may be slow because of an oversight in the initial assessment period; because the outcomes are not relevant or are too ambitious for the student; or because the teaching method is inappropriate. Evaluation can help you to identify accurately the source of difficulties and adjust the programme accordingly.

Often progress with the teaching programme is poorly recorded and the evaluation stage is neglected. It is useful to remember that ongoing record-keeping is vital for effective evaluation. Look over the details of the evaluation process for Angela's and David's teaching plans, and the sample record sheet used to monitor David's progress. You may find it useful to adapt or develop these processes in your own teaching.

Assessment	Goals or Objectives	Planning	Implementation	Evaluation
David cannot dress himself	David will put on his coat	Task Analysis identifies 10 steps Backward chaining to be used to master each step. Verbal prompts can be given. Reinforcer to be used: praise('well done – good boy') and hugs on completion of the step Mother to be the main teacher 2 sessions per day 3 attempts each session	Mother to put on David's coat working through the steps identified At the last step David to be verbally prompted to complete the task David to be praised on completion Record of performance to be made on chart	To review weekly

Figure 9: David's teaching plan

Record sheet

Step 10				
David to straighten lapels	4/3/96	5/3/96	6/3/96	7/3/96
i makes no attempt	√√	√√		
ii with verbal prompt	√	√√		
iii with non-verbal prompt		√√	√√	√√
iv completes the task unaided				√

Figure 10: Example of recording progress

Assessment	Goals or Objectives	Planning	Implementation	Evaluation
Angela has a high fat diet contributing to obesity	Long term goal: To maintain and under-stand the basis of a healthy diet	To provide cards that pictorially indicate low/ high fat content reinforcing the healthy/ unhealthy status by a √ or X	Teacher to introduce cards showing high and low fat foods	Angela will plan some meals using the cards to give examples of low fat nutritionally balanced meals
			Angela to place √s or Xs on the appropriate cards	
	Short term goals: 1. To identify a range of high and low fat foods 2. To plan a balanced meal	To explain basic nutritional information, i.e. the inclusion of protein carbohydrate	Teacher to demonstrate which combination of foods constitute a balanced meal, using starch, vitamins, etc. Picture cards of protein, e.g meat/ fish/beans Carbohydrate, e.g. potatoes/ rice Vitamins, e.g veg/fruit Starch, e.g cakes/ biscuits	

Figure 11: Angela's teaching plan

Summary

1 We have explored the importance of a positive learning climate and its impact on the learner.

2 We have identified the various stages of the teaching process and developed a systematic teaching plan for use with learners and their carers.

3 We have described some commonly used teaching methods and emphasised the importance of evaluating teaching outcomes.

Before you move on to Session Five you should check that you have achieved the learning objectives given at the beginning of the session and, if not, review the appropriate sections.

SESSION FIVE

Sexuality

Introduction

Human sexuality is a difficult and complex subject to understand. This session explores the impact of learning disability on the development and expression of sexuality in the context of life events. Social attitudes are considered, particularly in respect of the legal and moral right to a fulfilled life that applies to all citizens. Case material is used to illustrate key points in potentially difficult areas of sexuality.

Session objectives

When you have completed this session you should be able to:

- discuss the development and expression of sexuality

- evaluate the impact of learning disability on the development and expression of sexuality

- identify some common social attitudes towards sexuality in people with a learning disability

- analyse the important areas of carer support with respect to sexuality in people with a learning disability

- discuss the legal rights of the person with learning disability, with particular reference to fertility, marriage and pregnancy.

1: Exploring the term 'sexuality'

We can begin to develop our understanding of the challenges people with a learning disability face in their determination of the status of adulthood through an examination of the term 'sexuality'. Lion (1982) suggests that sexuality includes '...all those aspects of the human being that relate to being boy or girl, man or woman, and is an entity subject to lifelong dynamic change. Sexuality reflects our human characteristics, not solely our genital nature.' Craft (1987) offers the following perspective: 'Sex does not exist in a sealed box in the family home; it is as thoroughly woven into the social fabric of everyday life as the way we eat or do the shopping'.

ACTIVITY 73 — ALLOW 10 MINUTES

Make a list of some key words that come into your mind when you ask yourself the question 'What is sexuality, and how is it expressed?'.

Commentary

Your list may include other ideas but our lists probably cover the same broad areas.

hairstyle	perfume	relationships
clothes	gender roles	sexual acts
love	self-esteem	social activities
self-identity	masculinity	celibacy
image	arousal	femininity

As you can see, sexuality can be expressed in a variety of ways. Many things are vehicles for the expression of sexuality, including our appearance or image; there need not be a sexual act involved. What is apparent is that sexuality is an integral part of our lives, covering a broad spectrum ranging from attitudes to actual behaviours. Our sexuality is linked to our self-concept, self-esteem and personal identity and is crucially important.

ACTIVITY 74 — ALLOW 10 MINUTES

Reflect back on your own life and consider your ideas and knowledge about sexuality. What have been the key influences in creating your ideas? To what extent have these influences been obvious and to what extent have they been hidden?

Commentary

You probably recognise that various individuals, institutions and particular experiences have had varying degrees of influence. Influential people may include parents, teachers, peers, partners, television or film stars. Institutions that influence our ideas about sexuality could include the church or mosque or synagogue, school, workplace, clubs or organisations such as scouts and guides. Other influences may have come from television, books and magazines or particular events.

These are some of the key influences in the process of socialisation. The social norms that govern the expression of sexuality are learned mainly through the process of socialisation, in a way that often goes unnoticed at the time. Thus, if full access to the socialisation process is not available, opportunities for full sexual development and expression may be missed.

Having thought through some of your own experiences, it is now time to turn to the life chances of people with a learning disability.

ACTIVITY 75

ALLOW **10** MINUTES

Think of a particular person with a learning disability. To what extent are there similarities and differences between his or her process of socialisation and your own?

Commentary

Many of the opportunities that you will recognise from your experiences are rarely encountered by people with a learning disability. For example, their family life may have been disrupted by periods of residential care and leisure activities may have been constrained and focused into 'disabled' arenas rather than the varied social life available to most people. You will remember from the first three sessions that there are significant social limitations placed upon people with a learning disability as a consequence of negative stereotyping.

It is not uncommon for people with a learning disability to have a limited range of positive role models who can promote healthy development. The opportunities to clear up misunderstandings and confusions are limited by what Craft (1987) refers to as a conspiracy of silence. It is within this wall of silence that many people with a learning disability face emotional and physical changes.

2: Sexuality through the life cycle

Sexuality is frequently regarded as belonging to a specific and narrow life period, defined in law as beginning at 16 years (although full independence is only recognised at 18 years). The youth-focused culture in which we live would regard sexuality as ending as early as the fourth decade, an attitude that is beginning to change. Added to this is the tendency to ignore the sexuality of the infant and child, an issue that is of great significance for people who have a learning disability and who experience the status of eternal childhood.

ACTIVITY 76	ALLOW 10 MINUTES

Life cycle: *The opportunities that are present in an individual's life.*

Let us consider the early part of the **life cycle** to be made up of the following key stages: childhood; middle childhood; adolescence; early adult. Make brief notes for each stage of some of the key developments in relation to sexuality.

Commentary

I have identified the following key points which should broadly correspond with those you have noted.

Childhood	develop sensitivity to touch; learn sex differentiation, through play and clothing choices
Middle childhood	learn and internalise gender roles; gender identity is affirmed through peer associations in school life; develop predominantly same gender friendships

| Adolescence | learn masculine and feminine social roles; develop more mature relationships with both genders; peer group is a forum for exploring thoughts and feelings about sexuality and roles that eases the transition into adulthood; body changes become evident. |
| Early adult | selection of sexual partner; recognition of sexual identity; learn to live with a partner; rear children. |

We have seen that we learn about our sexuality through a series of progressive and developmental stages. The rules that govern behaviour regarded as appropriate for intimate relationships are learned through the various stages of our lives. The opportunities for this learning are limited for the person with a learning disability. This is exacerbated when there is a multiple handicap combining physical, sensory and intellectual impairments.

The degree of physical contact involved in different types of relationships is usually related to the level of sexual involvement. Yet there are many ways in which dependency encroaches on the privacy of people with a disability. Bathing, going to the toilet and giving suppositories, for example, all involve a high level of intimacy and to some extent are invasive actions. These are not commonly held experiences and their impact can be overlooked when considering the needs of the individual concerned.

William Horwood's novel about disability (1987) provides many insights into this area. The heroine experiences her first menstrual flow at the age of 16; finding herself covered in blood, she rejoices. Her grandmother initially reacts with concern and embarrassment but then reflects:

'And why after all should a girl who had been toileted by others all her life and who still ate food messily and always would, and who could not always control the spittle in her mouth, feel the slightest embarrassment about a period she had wanted to have for so long?'

3: Attitudes towards sexuality and learning disability

You will remember from Session One the exercise you carried out in relation to attitudes and learning disability. The next activity asks you to carry out a similar exercise, but this time with the focus on sexuality and disability.

ACTIVITY 77   ALLOW **10** MINUTES

Identify at least two ways in which other people's attitudes towards the sexuality of people with a learning disability can limit their sexual experience.

Commentary

I have listed four commonly held attitudes that can disadvantage people. People with a learning disability are frequently held to be:

- eternal children

- highly fertile (the opposite attitude is also held, that they are **infertile**)

- sexually promiscuous with poor self-control

- likely to be sexual perverts and possibly prey on children.

It is evident from these ideas that there is much confusion and contradiction in public attitudes. Many find it safer to consider people who are different as being asexual rather than deal with the issues that their needs may raise for us as carers or parents. The dependence and lack of autonomy that form part of the lifestyle of the person with a learning disability combine to create difficulties in the attainment of adult status.

This situation exists in the face of a significant amount of rhetoric that promotes the right of people with a learning disability to take up the status of adulthood. It is at that point in the building of personal relationships when development into some form of sexual partnership seems likely, that carers start to feel uncomfortable. I am sure that you will be familiar with some of these feelings of discomfort yourself.

ACTIVITY 78

ALLOW **10** MINUTES

Think about your experiences in relation to people with a learning disability. Identify some of the ways in which you may have felt some discomfort within the area of sexuality. Provide at least two examples.

Commentary

Our experiences cannot be exactly the same but it is likely that certain areas are common to many carers. These include:

- providing intimate care services for an adult member of the opposite sex

- assisting with the menstrual care of another woman

- masturbation

- becoming aware of your own embarrassment

- intimate care with the assistance of a member of the opposite sex.

In relation to disability, these feelings of discomfort can be avoided only at the cost of denying individuals their rights. Brown and Smith (1992) write:

> 'Women with learning difficulties can come up against a silence that makes it difficult for them to learn skills or develop a positive sense of their sexuality. Menstruation will be dealt with as a toileting chore rather than as a significant life event; they may not see 'valued' women managing their periods because to manage successfully in Western cultures means to manage in secret.'

The right to be a sexual being

Sexual development and the expression of sexuality for people with a learning disability have historically been suppressed and strictly controlled. You will recall from Session Two that the Victorian institutions evolved as a consequence of the moral panic experienced when it was feared that the 'mentally defective' population, with their perceived rampant sexuality, could overrun the country if left to reproduce at will. At a period when the influence of the eugenics movement was strong, the expansion of the institutions was rapid.

Sexuality played a key role, then, in the segregation and oppression of people with a learning disability. Fear and ignorance fuelled concern about people of low intelligence amongst the general population. As Burns (1993) points out, the term 'moral defective' was frequently used as synonymous with 'mental defective'. There are numerous accounts of women being committed to mental hospitals as a result of an illegitimate birth. The ethos of the day was repression and denial of sexuality, and remnants of this continue to impinge on the care practices of the present (Burns, 1993).

This legacy has led to:

- the systematic denial of rights and information for people with a learning disability

- the handing out of punitive measures

- segregation

- attempts to de-sexualise (using terms like boys and girls with adults).

Such practices in turn produce a distorted view of the sexuality of people with a learning disability in the public mind.

ACTIVITY 79　　　　　ALLOW 15 MINUTES

Think about the impact of past social attitudes on present care. Now consider some of the ways in which you might be able to turn the historical legacy around and create opportunities for the sexual growth of those in your care. Provide at least three examples of changes you would consider beneficial.

Commentary

However we might wish to change our practices, certain overriding rights of the individual must be highlighted and recognised if action is to be positive. Craft (1987) lists six rights of people with a learning disability, some of which will probably coincide with your own ideas. She states that people with a learning disability have:

1   The right to grow up: to be treated with the respect and dignity accorded to adults.

2   The right to know: to have access to as much information about themselves and their bodies, and those of other people, their emotions, appropriate social behaviour as they can assimilate.

3   The right to be sexual and to make and break relationships.

4   The right not to be at the mercy of the individual sexual attitudes of different care givers.

5   The right not to be sexually abused.

6   The right to humane and dignified environments.

As you can surmise from the evident discrepancies between these stated rights and the traditions of care, a major change in our attitudes is necessary. During a workshop on sexuality, I remember a carer providing insights into some of the dilemmas faced. Support was being offered to a young woman who was beginning to be aware of her body and the development of sexual feelings. The care staff were trying to help her, but their work was almost undone when one particular carer decided that such discussion was 'dirty' and 'offensive' and almost destroyed the young woman's self-esteem.

We will now consider some of the ways in which carers can assist in the positive development of sexuality.

4: Analysing and supporting sex education needs

ACTIVITY 80   ALLOW 10 MINUTES

1   Read the case study below about Kelly Roberts.

2   Make a list of any concerns you may have identified for Kelly.

Kelly Roberts

Kelly is 27 years old and lives in a group home with three other women. There is a care worker who comes in the morning and another who works for two hours in the evening and for a few extra hours at weekends.

Kelly attends the Adult Training Centre (ATC) where she packs cards. She also attends some skill training sessions – cookery and basic literacy. She lived in the local hospital for people with a learning disability from the age of eight until four years ago. She was admitted after her mother suffered a breakdown in health and no longer felt able to cope with Kelly at home.

Kelly can wash herself. She needs reminding to take a bath and requires closer supervision during menstruation. She dresses herself but has little idea about clothes sense, age appropriateness or seasonal considerations.

She cannot read but can recognise certain words and labels.

Kelly is very friendly and sociable. She will chat to anyone – at a superficial level she will communicate well, giving the impression of being more capable than she actually is. Until recently she has had a limited social life, mainly based around an evening club at the ATC. She goes shopping and for walks with the other women in the house. She attends the local Catholic church regularly.

About four months ago, Kelly became friendly with George, a 40-year-old man from the ATC. She appears to be rather dominated by George, who makes all the decisions about what they do. The friendship is mainly conducted at the ATC and the evening club, although George has visited Kelly at home a few times over the last month.

When asked about George, Kelly says they are in love but she seems to have little notion about relationships. It is almost as if she is acting out a part based on characters from the TV.

The care workers are now concerned because Kelly has told them that George wants her to have a baby. She says that she would like a baby, but not just yet.

Commentary

You probably listed a range of concerns and needs that are apparent from Kelly's story. I have suggested five main areas :

● personal health

● bodily functions and changes, including menstruation

- relationships
- assertiveness
- sexual intercourse, contraception and pregnancy.

Now that we have identified some needs, further information gathering is required to help promote the developments necessary for Kelly to grow towards full adulthood. One strategy that is commonly used in health and social care environments is to consider the holistic needs of the individual (Beck, Rawlins and Williams, 1988).

ACTIVITY 81   ALLOW 15 MINUTES

Using the headings below, identify the actual areas of help and support that Kelly requires.

Physical

Social

Emotional

Intellectual

Spiritual

Commentary

I recognised the following areas that require some development and input in this case.

Physical: work to be undertaken around personal health and hygiene. There are also issues relating to pregnancy and childbirth that will need to be addressed at some stage.

Social: Kelly's understanding of and ability to form relationships is lacking, due to her lengthy period of institutional care. She needs to explore the different sorts of relationships and what is expected within them. Her contacts with ordinary lifestyles are few and there are few role models for her to observe. It is not surprising that she gleans what she can from the television.

Emotional: it is unlikely that Kelly will have been involved in much personal development work before and it is very likely that she will have many misunderstandings that need to be explored before she is wholly able to undertake new learning.

Intellectual: Kelly's understanding and management of her menstrual cycle needs developing. Linked to this is her need to understand other aspects of bodily functions and changes she has experienced. In view of her disclosure that George wants a baby, she will need information and advice about intercourse, reproduction, contraception, pregnancy and childbirth.

Spiritual: what is worrying about Kelly's situation is her vulnerability. Her lack of preparation leaves her ill-equipped for a life of independence and self-determination. There are indications that Kelly has difficulty making choices, and some assertiveness training could be necessary. All of these add to the need for her self-esteem to be improved and for her sense of self-identity to become established.

Overall, if her relationship with George is to develop positively, it is important that these issues are addressed very soon.

ACTIVITY 82　　　　ALLOW **10** MINUTES

What specific kinds of support do you think are necessary to enable Kelly to meet her needs? List your suggestions below.

Commentary

I have identified three main areas and I would hope that your suggestions are broadly along these lines.

Kelly needs the support of a skilled person who has expertise in this area of work. This will be someone who is comfortable discussing aspects of sexuality. If you are unsure as to whether you are sufficiently skilled in this area, then involve someone who is trained in this field.

Kelly will need to feel that she is being helped and supported and not that the agenda is to end her relationship with George. This will be aided by the development of a trusting relationship between carers and herself.

Some of the issues could be addressed with both Kelly *and* George if this seemed appropriate. It would be helpful if George's personal development coincided with Kelly's.

One of the frequent problems faced by carers is that they have to react to problematic situations that could have been avoided if a proper assessment of need had occurred earlier. All too often, issues relating to sexuality are not addressed unless the individual actually demonstrates an interest in expressing their sexuality. It is this expression of sexuality that is often viewed as a problem. Any inappropriate form of expression is considered an even bigger problem. Problems are often dealt with by suppressing them – the very strategy that has created many of the difficulties faced by people with a learning disability in the first place. They need our support in asserting their rights.

5: Human rights and adulthood

The United Nations 'Declaration on the Rights of Mentally Retarded Persons' (1971) stated that individuals with a learning disability should, where feasible, have the same rights as other citizens. As a member of the United Nations, Britain should be implementing the Declaration. In reality this is often made difficult by a number of factors. Conflicting legislation which is contrary to the aims of the Declaration can present obstacles, as can a range of social policies, economic constraints and prejudiced attitudes.

Any discussion on adulthood would not be complete without some consideration of the legal and ethical dilemmas that are raised when people with a learning disability try to assert their rights. We will pursue our discussion using the case study of Kelly Roberts but adding different scenarios that will broaden the scope of our problem-solving.

ACTIVITY 83   ALLOW 15 MINUTES

Read the following addition to Kelly's case study. What issues are raised in this scenario? Identify possible solutions for this dilemma.

> As **Kelly's** relationship with George progresses, she asks permission to stay over with him for the weekend so that they can sleep together. The staff agree to this, provided that she uses contraception. In the meantime they arrange an appointment with her GP to discuss the possibility of a sterilisation operation.

Commentary

There are a number of issues here, not least of which is that Kelly is endeavouring to adopt an adult role but is placed in a child-like relationship to her carers by having to ask permission for what the average adult would consider a personal decision. Furthermore, the controlled nature of her lifestyle becomes clear when significant and powerful people in her life make a major decision to discuss her body with another person without her consent. Her relationship is permitted only with restrictions or provisions. These may turn out to be eminently sensible decisions, but they are made as though her sex education was insufficient or the carers did not trust her. The carer role here is very much one of parent or guardian, with Kelly's role being that of an older child.

The decision to prepare for future events through a possible sterilisation is somewhat drastic, but this does happen through the actions of formal and informal carers. Do you remember the case of Jeanette, a young woman whose mother successfully petitioned the high court to allow her to be sterilised as she was concerned that her daughter may become sexually active and that she would be unable to care for a child unsupported. Interestingly, when sterilisation is the focus, it is always the woman who is the prospective patient. There are no examples of men with learning disability being submitted to sterilisation as a form of contraception. The main area of concern here however is not so much gender as the need to reflect on the question of whose convenience is met by sterilisation.

ACTIVITY 84   ALLOW 25 MINUTES

Read the next scenario and then try to imagine yourself in the roles of Kelly, her brother and the carers. Now consider the main concerns attendant on each role. (The legal position is that there are no laws restricting marriage in this instance if the Registrar is satisfied that Kelly knows what she is doing.)

Case study

> **Kelly** announces that she and her boyfriend George wish to marry. When her brother, who is married with children, hears about this he is very unhappy and makes clear his intention to prevent the marriage going ahead. He remembers vividly some of the traumas of his early childhood, when his mother was exhausted by caring continuously for Kelly. He was relieved that Kelly's future seemed safe and secure when she was admitted to the home. The care staff are happy about the marriage, with reservations, but feel that they are placed in a difficult position between Kelly and her brother.

Kelly

Her brother

The care staff

Commentary

Kelly may find that she is having to ask so many different people for permission – the care staff, her family, George's family – that she could become confused as to her own desires. Kelly may have dreamed of a wonderful wedding with a beautiful dress and her own house, but not know how to achieve all of this. If Kelly has been supported by others in her relationship with George, and has shown that she understands her own sexuality, then she may well feel that she has been betrayed if the care staff support her brother, or if her family prevents her marriage. She recognises that she will need support, but feels that whatever happens George will be there and their love will prevail.

Her brother is outraged that Kelly is being placed in a vulnerable position and could be removed from the security of the residential home to an unsatisfactory flat in a poor area of the city. He feels that George is too old and that he is taking advantage of his sister. His view is that the care staff have been remiss in their duty by letting this situation arise. If necessary, Kelly should be removed from the ATC and kept under closer supervision. Kelly's brother remembers the distress his mother experienced when Kelly had to be put into care and he is afraid that outside a residential home he may be obliged to support her. He feels that he cannot do this as he has a wife and children of his own who are his first concern. Therefore, this marriage must be prevented at all costs. He is prepared to take legal action to demonstrate that Kelly is not fit to make such a decision for herself.

The care staff have been worried about something like this happening for some time and feel some conflict as to where their responsibilities lie. They feel that they do have some responsibility towards Kelly's family and are conscious that they themselves could be seen as being *in loco parentis* should anything go wrong. Aside from the emotional and physical issues, there are the practical concerns of financing this wedding. Without the support of her family, Kelly cannot have the wedding she dreams about. With Kelly on one side and her brother on the other, they may find themselves pressured into taking sides. The safest recourse may well be to agree with the brother as this would maintain the status quo. However, this would rather make a mockery of all their efforts to create independence and promote the rights of those in their care.

In the short term there are no satisfactory answers here. It is necessary to take a long-term view and recognise that none of our lives occur in a vacuum. If, as carers, we are to make some changes in the standards of living and the opportunities available to those in our care, we must do two things. First, we need to be prepared to take reasonable risks. Second, we need to involve all elements of an individual's social life from an early stage. If parents wish to limit the extent of an able person's adulthood, that person can 'vote with their feet' and leave home. However, the greater the degree of impairment, the more difficult it is to make statements of independence. It is therefore imperative that long-term planning involves those significant parties at a stage when they can appreciate the extent of the personal development of that individual.

ACTIVITY 85   ALLOW 15 MINUTES

> Kelly has been feeling very tired and complaining of being generally under the weather for some weeks. She was taken to the GP who suggested a pregnancy test, which proved positive. The care staff feel that it would totally inappropriate for Kelly to bring up a child and decide that she should be persuaded to have an abortion.

Abortion is an emotive subject and as such is often avoided. What, in your view, are the key issues that arise from this scenario?

Commentary

The use of abortion as a preventative or contraceptive measure is fairly common. The rules regarding consent to treatment are the same for Kelly as for anyone else. However, this is often overlooked, particularly in a care environment where it is often assumed that carers are the correct people to make informed decisions, rather than the individuals concerned. The status of the individual as a child rather than an adult, due to their need for support, reinforces the tendency for carers to make crucial decisions unilaterally. Linked to this is the notion that people who have no diagnosed learning disability, such as carers, are better able to predict problems and so are entitled to make such decisions.

In Kelly's case there is the added dimension of religion. She is a Catholic and as such has strong reservations about abortion. Such concerns are frequently ignored in the care area and this could lead to Kelly experiencing much spiritual pain if an abortion was carried out. It is Kelly's stated wish that she wants to have a baby at some time in the future.

There are positive instances of couples who have a learning disability successfully caring for a child. They are highly critical of some of the support they receive. They suggest that carers should listen to the parents and take advice from them on how to help effectively. One couple who came to present a paper at a conference I attended had experienced severe prejudice from some carers who were, after all, being paid to support them. They exercised their right to change the service agents and found support from carers who were positive in their approaches. The Victorian notions of the eugenics movement and the rapid breeding of a 'defective race' are apparently not so far removed when some of the prejudices evident in care environments today are considered.

We have seen that, when a learning disability adds to a person's vulnerability, then the recognition of adulthood becomes very difficult. Add to this the secrecy that surrounds sexuality in our culture, and it can seem irresponsible on the part of a carer to expose the person with a learning disability to all the possible problems. But taking reasonable risks is part of adulthood, and recognising the human rights of vulnerable groups is an essential part of modern care developments.

There are no neat answers to the dilemmas created when considering the sexuality of people who have a learning disability. You are advised to discuss these and other issues that may have occurred to you with your colleagues. On the whole, they will welcome such discussion, as we all have some reservations about the 'correctness' of our approaches in this area. There is a great deal of difficulty in working within an area so set about with ethical, moral and legal dilemmas. Each case is unique and there is no text book with the right answers. The carer must work with the individual to identify the right decision for that person at that time.

Summary

1 We have attempted to understand some of the key aspects of human sexuality and their impact on the physical and emotional development of people with a learning disability.

2 We have enhanced our understanding of this subject through study of case material.

3 We have considered the broad area of social attitudes about the sexuality of people with a learning disability.

4 We have explored carers' experiences and responsibilities regarding this right, and considered how they can assist in the positive development of sexuality in the people for whom they care.

Before you move on to Session Six you should check that you have achieved the learning objectives given at the beginning of this session and, if not, review the appropriate sections.

Management of challenging behaviour

Introduction

This session explores forms of behaviour that are challenging both to the individual and to the carer. We define the term 'challenging behaviour' and describe its components. Drawing on personal experience, you will examine your own definitions and compare them with those cited in the literature. We investigate some of the suggested causes of challenging behaviour and the way it impacts upon the person's lifestyle. The concept of dual diagnosis and the development of a framework for integrated functioning is discussed. The session concludes with an overview of a therapeutic approach to challenging behaviour.

Session objectives

When you have completed this session, you should be able to:

- define challenging behaviour and discuss its characteristics

- describe a range of possible causes of challenging behaviour in learning disability

- consider the integrated functioning of the individual in terms of a theoretical framework of their physical, intellectual, social, emotional and spiritual dimensions

- discuss the lifestyle and social implications of challenging behaviour upon the individual with learning disability

- describe and discuss a behaviouristic therapeutic approach to challenging behaviour, with special reference to functional analysis of the behaviour using the behavioural analysis (ABC) chart.

1: Defining challenging behaviour

'Challenging behaviour' is an all-embracing term used to describe or diagnose certain maladaptive behaviours that people with a learning disability exhibit for a number of reasons. The term is relatively new in the field of learning disabilities. The types of behaviour that we will examine used to be referred to as 'difficult behaviours', 'disruptive behaviours', or 'problem behaviours'. In using this type of terminology, it was implied that the individual was the problem. This created a vicious circle, in that by labelling people as problems, they are perceived by others as problems, which in turn influences how they are regarded in society and cared for by service providers.

It is important to be able to distinguish between behaviours that may be perceived as a problem, and behaviours which justify a diagnosis of challenging behaviour. Behaviour which is a problem to others because of its annoying or irritating nature, for example, is not necessarily a challenging behaviour. For example, people with a learning disability may have communication deficits, and their attempts to communicate their needs may present as inappropriate behaviours.

Let us consider, then, what the term 'challenging behaviour' means to us. In whatever capacity we work within in the field of learning disabilities, we will find that this label is applied to many in our client group.

ACTIVITY 86 — ALLOW 10 MINUTES

What does the term 'challenging behaviour' mean to you? It may help if you think about behaviours exhibited by some of your own clients. Now list those behaviours which you know are commonly described as 'challenging behaviour'.

Commentary

You are likely to have included on your list behaviours such as: headbanging; skin picking/scratching; aggression/attacking others; hyperactivity; biting self or others; throwing objects; tearing clothes; kicking; stealing food; attention seeking; shouting/screaming.

This list is by no means exhaustive, but it provides us with a basis on which to consider our definition of challenging behaviour.

Mansell (1994) uses a definition by Emerson et al. (1987) in which challenging behaviour is defined as:

'behaviour which presents a serious risk to the physical safety of the individual or others around them, or which prevents the individual taking part in everyday life in the community.'

From this we can identify three clear categories of challenging behaviour:

- those which present a serious risk to the physical safety of the individual

- those which present a serious risk to the physical safety of others

- those which restrict the individual from taking part in everyday life.

ACTIVITY 87　　　　　　　　ALLOW **10** MINUTES

Try to assign each of the behaviours you listed in the previous activity to one or more of the three categories above.

Commentary

Examples of behaviours presenting a serious risk to the individual are headbanging and self-biting. Kicking, throwing and biting put others at risk, while all the behaviours listed are likely to be detrimental to social acceptance. Hyperactive and aggressive behaviours can fall into all three categories.

Definition and categorisation of challenging behaviour may be useful for diagnosis, but it can give a misleading picture. It has been argued that the term does little to alter perceptions of the individual and some have argued for a change in emphasis away from the individual to the individual's environment. Derbyshire and Whitaker (1990) have suggested that challenging behaviour is a challenge for the environment. This view is supported by Flemming (1993) who considers that the strength of the term 'challenging behaviour' lies in its relationship to both behaviour and the environment. The behaviour therefore should not be seen as challenging because of its adverse consequences, but rather as a challenge to the service providers to give the individual good quality care.

2: Causes of challenging behaviour

Understanding the *causes* of challenging behaviour is important if we are to implement the appropriate care strategies which will provide the individual with a good quality of life. The relationship between the causes of challenging behaviour and appropriate therapeutic interventions will become clearer as you work through the session.

ACTIVITY 88

List some of the reasons why people with a learning disability might exhibit a challenging behaviour.

Commentary

Your list may have included some of the following:

- the effect of an underlying medical condition
- effects of medication
- frustration resulting from communication problems or poor mobility/coordination and insufficient external stimulation.

This subdivision of causes of challenging behaviour into three types is common in the literature on this subject. These are:

- biological/organic causes
- social/environmental causes
- psychological causes/learned behaviours.

Let us now consider each in turn.

Biological/organic causes

Much of the literature on this cause of challenging behaviour in learning disability has focused on self-injurious behaviour (SIB). Here researchers have found definite links with certain clinical syndromes. There is, for example, well-documented evidence (Christie et al., 1982) to suggest that people with Lesch–Nyhan syndrome develop self-biting behaviours which result in severe damage to lips, hands and fingers. Other syndromes associated with SIB include de Lange syndrome and Gilles de la Tourette syndrome.

The incidence and severity of the challenging behaviour is directly related to the degree of learning disability that the individual exhibits. In other words, the greater the learning disability, the more severe the challenging behaviour. A severe learning disability impedes memory and reasoning, so inhibiting problem-solving abilities. This can lead to frustration and to an increase in inappropriate and self-abusive behaviours.

These syndromes are rare and it is unlikely that many of us have come across them in the course of our working lives. One condition that we are all aware of, however, is that of autism. There is a growing body of evidence to suggest that people with autism or autistic tendencies do exhibit a higher degree of challenging behaviour, and that there is a strong link with the degree of learning disability.

Social/environmental causes

Return for a moment to the last activity and look at your list of possible causes of challenging behaviour. It is likely that much of your list falls under the heading of environmental causes. Our environment is a crucial element in determining our behaviour.

ACTIVITY 89 ALLOW **15** MINUTES

Imagine for a moment that you are unable to communicate with the people who are there to care for you. Your carers misguidedly believe that they are providing you with sensory stimulation by turning on the radio. Unfortunately the radio stays on from the moment you wake to the moment you go to bed, seven days a week.

1 How might you feel about this situation?

2 Without the ability to communicate your feelings, how might you react?

3 If you start to exhibit inappropriate behaviours what label might be applied to you?

4 Can you identify some of those behaviours in any of the people you care for at the moment?

Commentary

It is all too easy to imagine how quickly frustration would build up in this situation, both in response to the circumstances themselves and to your inability to influence them. In people with a learning disability, behaviour arising in an attempt to draw attention to their plight could all too easily prove inappropriate, but it is likely to be the individuals themselves who are labelled troublesome, difficult or challenging. You may be able to identify this behaviour in someone you have cared for. Harris (1993) identified the communication problems of people with a learning disability as a major contributory factor in challenging behaviour.

Self-stimulatory hypothesis: *A theory which suggests that every person needs a certain level of stimulation. People with a learning disability may be under-stimulated because of the nature of their environment.*

There are many other environmental factors which could contribute towards challenging behaviour. The **self-stimulatory hypothesis** is a theory common in the literature on the subject. This suggests that each person needs a certain level of stimulation. People with a learning disability may be under-stimulated because of the nature of their environment. In her ground-breaking book *The Empty Hours,* Oswin (1971) illustrated the effect of sterile environments on disabled children's cognitive development. She refers to boredom, loneliness, lack of toys, occupations and tactile stimulation. Similar observations can be made about adults with a learning disability, who when placed in this position may attempt self-stimulation. This can take the form of self-injury and these behaviours may in time provide their own reinforcement.

Psychological causes/learned behaviours

Although there are a number of theories of social learning, the impact of behaviourism on our understanding of the learning process has been profound and the term **'conditioning'** has become part of the language of psychology. The powerful theories offered by Gestalt psychology suggest that learning is achieved through a stimulus–response (SR) approach. In simple terms this says that certain behaviour is tied to a particular stimulus.

Conditioning: *A type of learning where a response results from a neutral stimulus, which previously had been repeatedly presented in conjunction with the stimulus that originally elicited the response.*

Conditioning theories suggest that behaviours are learned as a result of the consequences of their occurrence – in effect, because of positive and negative **reinforcement** (Lowe et al., 1993). Mackintosh (1984) argues that conditioning can be thought of as detecting and learning about relationships between events.

Reinforcement: *Rewarding behaviour – making it more likely to happen again.*

ACTIVITY 90

ALLOW **10** MINUTES

Think about the way in which you have developed a particular aspect of your behaviour. Think of a type of behaviour which you know to be appropriate, and consider the following:

1   How did you acquire the behaviour?

2   How were you shown this behaviour by others?

3   What responses were given to you when you attempted to behave appropriately?

4   What responses were given to you when you could not or would not perform this behaviour correctly?

Commentary

Childhood experiences instantly come to mind. When children are first old enough to eat meals with the rest of the family, they have to learn appropriate mealtime behaviour from those around them. There is usually an element of teaching, but also much imitation. Adherence to appropriate behaviour codes may be rewarded – perhaps by being allowed to stay up a bit later – while transgressions may be punished, say by having to leave the table or by having a privilege withdrawn.

Throughout the process of our development people offer us both positive and negative reinforcement. Challenging behaviour can also develop in people with learning disability as a result of the inappropriate and inadvertent use of reinforcers. We shall return to this issue later in this session.

3: A framework for integrated functioning

The aetiology of challenging behaviour can involve more than the physical dimension. If we consider again the work of Oswin (1971), for example, it becomes clear that behaviour emanates from a wide spectrum of human functioning. We have also discovered how a diagnosis of learning disability can in itself lead to lost opportunities, labelling and stigma. It can be argued, therefore, that a diagnosis of learning disability combined with a diagnosis of challenging behaviour is a dual handicap, with far-reaching implications for the person's quality of life.

In discussing these issues we will use a health model proposed by Beck, Rawlins and Williams (1988) to identify the detrimental effects that challenging behaviour can have upon the individual. We shall then be in a position to consider how these negative factors can be turned around to achieve positive gains in the individual's quality of life.

Beck, Rawlins and Williams' (1988) framework has its origins in nursing and health, but is equally valuable in other disciplines. They emphasise the 'integrative functioning of the client's physical, intellectual, social, emotional and spiritual dimensions'. Each person is considered as a whole with many factors contributing to health and illness. Although health and illness are specifically referred to in this quote, we could adapt it to read 'factors which contribute to the person's quality of life'. Beck, Rawlins and Williams go on to say that 'the recognition of all human dimensions encourages a balanced and whole view of the person. Each facet of an individual is important and contributes to the quality of life experienced'. For people with a dual diagnosis of learning disability and challenging behaviour, there will be many factors that impinge upon their quality of life. By definition, there will be some intellectual and social deficit; in many cases, physical problems will contribute to limiting of opportunity and unsatisfactory life experiences may lead to emotional difficulties.

Figure 12 illustrates Beck, Rawlins and Williams' framework.

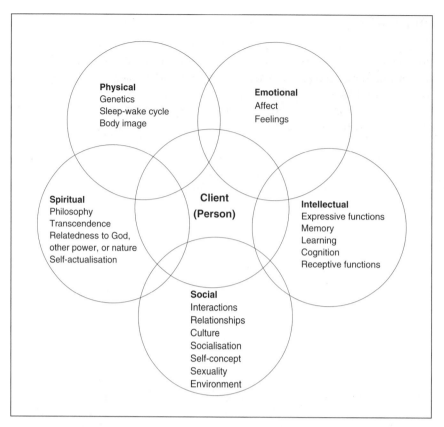

Figure 12: The Beck, Rawlins and Williams framework

Apply the Beck, Rawlins and Williams framework to yourself by listing some of the factors which you feel are important to your own quality of life under the headings below.

Physical	Social	Intellectual	Emotional	Spiritual

Commentary

I imagine your list will be wide-ranging and will have made you think hard about the columns specific factors should be placed in. Many will fit into more than one column. There is no problem with this, as it serves to remind us of the integrative nature of the framework.

I would now like to move the focus from you and consider these factors in relation to the client with challenging behaviour.

ACTIVITY 92 ALLOW 20 MINUTES

Read the following case study and then identify the factors which impinge on this person's lifestyle using the template below.

Case study

David is a 28-year-old man who was admitted to a large hospital for people with a learning disability when he was 5 years old. He moved from the institution three years ago to live in a small group home catering to the needs of five residents who all present a challenge to the service.

David is 6ft 2ins tall and of stocky build. He has no verbal communication skills except for a high-pitched scream and a loud grunting noise. He has limited self-help and social skills, is able to dress himself only with constant verbal assistance, and is incontinent of urine. He can feed himself with a spoon. He has a tendency to steal the food of other residents, particularly those residents smaller than himself.

David is prone to aggressive outbursts, physically attacking smaller residents and staff alike. He also throws objects and furniture.

David did attend adult education classes at the local college of further education, but was excluded due to his aggressive behaviour. At present he has no daytime occupation.

Physical	Social	Intellectual	Emotional	Spiritual

Commentary

You will see from your lists that David's opportunities are severely limited because of his challenging behaviour. Under the physical heading, you will probably have noted David's size, which can promote a sense of fear and intimidation in others, particularly if he is exhibiting aggressive behaviours. Because of his past experiences and behaviour, David's socialisation processes will be severely affected. He has already lost his place at day services as a consequence of his behaviour. He has a reputation for aggression and staff may be reluctant to escort him on outings or visits to the local community facilities. This will affect him intellectually, as he will miss out on the normal learning opportunities for the development of self-help and social skills. The emotional effect of all this on David may be to isolate him further and create feelings of rejection, boredom, and frustration. On a spiritual level, if he continues to be restricted he may well develop a poor self-esteem, and miss out on opportunities to feel valued.

To comment on this activity I have discussed only one factor, working it through the whole integrative process of becoming a valued community member. You could go through this process with all the factors that you have identified. What has been created for David is a vicious circle.

ACTIVITY 93

ALLOW 5 MINUTES

Refer back to the final activity in Session Two, and then draw a vicious circle based on David's case study, showing the lost opportunities that David will experience.

Commentary

You have produced a visual representation of the scenario outlined above. The emotional effects described, for example, are likely to lead to even more aggressive and challenging behaviour which will further worsen his reputation and make it even more likely that David will miss out on learning and social opportunities.

You have learned that having a challenging behaviour can have a profound effect upon an individual's developmental processes. It can create a climate of lost opportunities, with the potential for an escalation in the degree of the challenging behaviour. We now explore ways in which we can try to arrest these behaviours.

4: A therapeutic approach to challenging behaviour

Although there are several therapeutic options available for managing challenging behaviours, I intend to examine one in depth, as it is possibly the most widely used technique in the field of learning disabilities. This technique seeks to assess and analyse the antecedents and consequences of an individual's behaviour.

Behaviourists argue that an action is determined by its consequences. These actions may be very mild to start with, but if the desired consequences are achieved by the client then the action is positively reinforced and may intensify.

ACTIVITY 94   ALLOW 15 MINUTES

Read the following scenario and then answer the questions that follow.

A client sits quietly in the living room rocking to and fro in his chair. This is his normal pattern of behaviour during the day. One day, while the staff are busily going about their tasks, the client stands up from his chair, picks it up and throws it across the room. All the staff on the shift come running to see what has happened, and unthinkingly make a fuss of the client. They settle him back down into his chair and he remains quiet for the rest of the day. The following day the client repeats his actions.

1 Explain how this client has been given reinforcement.

2 How may this behaviour be justified in terms of attention seeking?

3 What is this client learning from the consequences of his behaviour?

Commentary

In this scenario, the staff have inadvertently given positive reinforcement to the client's actions by providing fuss and attention, which he may feel he lacks, in response to the challenging behaviour. The client will therefore learn that this type of behaviour is both stimulating and, apparently, the key to gaining the attention of his carers, and so will continue to repeat the behaviour.

Reed and Head (1993) argue that 'challenging behaviours almost by definition are guaranteed to provoke a response from carers' and that 'carers are more likely to respond to undesirable behaviours'. Unless situations are handled appropriately, therefore, the inappropriate behaviour is likely to escalate.

Functional analysis:
An approach which aims to discover the pre-disposing factors to challenging behaviour and to understand how the inappropriate behaviour serves the individual.

One behaviourist method of intervention in this cycle is that of **functional analysis.** The aim of functional analysis is to discover the pre-disposing factors to challenging behaviour and to understand how the inappropriate behaviour serves the individual. Once this is understood, replacement behaviours which are appropriate to enhancing the quality of life for the individual can be introduced as the challenging behaviour is eradicated. If we do not attempt to understand how the behaviours serve the individual, any form of intervention we make in caring will eventually break down and we will risk a recurrence of the behaviours in question.

Functional analysis, then, is about providing a thorough assessment of behaviour, and determining appropriate strategies for intervention. A number of strategies are employed to assess the relationship between client and environment. The behavioural analysis chart is a very widely used strategy. You may have seen or assisted in recording behaviours for a behavioural analysis chart before. Referred to as an **ABC chart**, this records the chain of events associated with the behaviour which is inappropriate (commonly referred to as the target behaviour). Recordings are made about the:

- Antecedent, the conditions which existed before the behaviour occurred, to identify pre-disposing factors for the behaviour

- Behaviour, explaining in detail exactly what behaviour occurred

- Consequences, providing detailed information about what happened as a result of the behaviour.

ACTIVITY 95   ALLOW 30 MINUTES

Ideally, you need access to a client for this activity. If this is not possible, either think back to a client you have worked with in the past, or discuss the activity with a colleague who is currently working with a suitable client.

During the course of your practice, you may already have observed many instances of inappropriate behaviour. Using one such example, try to complete the ABC chart below. It may be useful to try and document a number of instances where the target behaviour is apparent.

Antecedent	Behaviour	Consequence

Commentary

How did you get on? Were you able to plot the progress from antecedent to consequences? Let us consider for a moment how you have actually described the events that occurred. *Figure 13* is an example using the scenario from the last activity. (I have elaborated slightly to provide this example.)

Antecedent	Behaviour	Consequence
Day 1		
9.00 a.m. Client alone rocking to and fro in chair.	Client stands up, picks up chair and throws it across the room.	Staff run to client, provide attention.
Day 2		
9.30 a.m. Client alone rocking to and fro in his chair.	Client screams, picks up his chair and throws it across the room.	Staff run to client, provide attention.
2.30 p.m. Client alone rocking to and fro in his chair.	Client screams, picks up his chair and throws it across the room, injuring another client.	Staff run to client, provide attention.
Day 3		
9.00 a.m. Client quiet in chair rocking to and fro.	Client screams, picks up his chair and throws it across the room.	Staff run to client, provide attention.
1.30 p.m. Client sitting quietly in chair rocking to and fro.	Client screams, runs up and down the living room, turns over a chair occupied by another client, causing injury and distress.	Staff run to client and attempt to calm him down, attention given.
7.30 p.m. Client quietly in chair rocking to and fro.	Client picks up his chair and throws it across the room.	Staff provide attention.

Figure 13: Example of an ABC chart

It can be seen from this simple example that a pattern of undesirable behaviour is emerging which is escalating in severity. Before the first incident, the client's normal pattern of behaviour was sitting alone rocking to and fro in his chair. Thus the client was already showing signs of self-stimulatory behaviour, i.e. rocking. However, this was no longer meeting his optimal level of stimulation.

Within the pattern of behaviour being established, the client is learning that if he exhibits certain types of behaviours he will gain what to him is a pleasurable consequence. Attention given to him immediately after the demonstration of the undesirable behaviour is his reward, and consequently reinforces the undesirable behaviour.

Once this analysis has been completed, the care team are in a position to intervene. In this example, the intervention would aim to establish a pattern of behaviour which provides the client with the attention he seeks without his having to demonstrate undesirable behaviour.

ACTIVITY 96

ALLOW 10 MINUTES

Examine the behavioural analysis chart that you completed for the last activity and then answer the following questions.

1   What patterns of behaviour have been established?

2   What rewards to the client are acting as reinforcers to the target behaviour?

3   Can you suggest any strategies for managing this behaviour?

Commentary

Naturally, the answers to these questions will depend on the precise details of your case study. However, I hope you can see from this activity how successful therapeutic intervention is crucially dependent upon analysis of the source and consequences of the behaviour, as well as the exact details of the behaviour itself.

The ABC chart is only one method of providing adequate data for a functional analysis, and it is not without its critics. Furthermore, behaviourism is only one of the approaches used to ameliorate challenging behaviour, although it has been widely adopted in the field of learning disabilities. As the knowledge base extends in this field, alternative approaches are gaining momentum. I would like to conclude this session by recommending that you do some further reading in this area, so that you may explore these methods in greater depth at your leisure.

Summary

1 We have defined challenging behaviour, explored its components and categorised types of behaviour that challenge both the individual and the carer.

2 We have considered your personal definitions of challenging behaviour and compared them with those cited in the literature reviewed.

4 We have investigated some of the suggested causes of challenging behaviour and discussed the ways these affect the person's lifestyle and quality of life.

5 We have explored the concept of dual diagnosis and the development of a framework for integrated functioning.

6 Finally, we have considered a therapeutic approach to challenging behaviour.

LEARNING REVIEW

Now you have completed this unit, you will have extended your knowledge and critical understanding of the social context of caring for people with a learning disability. You will find it useful to work through the self-assessment questionnaire. This will help you to identify where you have made good progress, and where you still feel less confident. You will find it helpful to compare the completed review with the learning profile which you filled in at the beginning of the unit.

	Not at all	Partly	Quite well	Very well

Session One

I can:

- review some common causes of learning disability and significant associated conditions including epilepsy and cerebral palsy ☐ ☐ ☐ ☐
- analyse the social impact of learning disability on the family ☐ ☐ ☐ ☐
- discuss the significance of sibling rivalry in relation to learning ☐ ☐ ☐ ☐
- disability ☐ ☐ ☐ ☐
- analyse the language of disability ☐ ☐ ☐ ☐
- discuss the impact of disability on the individual's life chances. ☐ ☐ ☐ ☐

Session Two

I can:

- review the history of care of people with learning disabilities ☐ ☐ ☐ ☐
- relate this to the prevailing attitudes of the time ☐ ☐ ☐ ☐
- describe the impact of institutionalisation on individual development ☐ ☐ ☐ ☐
- explain the current structure of care provision ☐ ☐ ☐ ☐
- explain the significance of the mixed economy of care. ☐ ☐ ☐ ☐

Session Three

I can:

- define what is meant by the term 'normalisation' ☐ ☐ ☐ ☐

	Not at all	Partly	Quite well	Very well

Session Three *continued*

- explain the origin of the concept and its early implications for institutional care — □ □ □ □
- evaluate normalisation as a principle for practice, and discuss its role in the move to community care for learning disability — □ □ □ □
- identify the impact of unconscious prejudice on the development of human services — □ □ □ □
- explain the concept of a conservative corollary to the principle of normalisation and its importance — □ □ □ □
- identify key accomplishments that services should try to achieve on behalf of users and apply this to an individual case study — □ □ □ □
- review the process of audit for the care environment in relation to the quality of care and the promotion of a 'normal' lifestyle. — □ □ □ □

Session Four

I can:

- evaluate the processes of teaching and learning — □ □ □ □
- plan, implement and evaluate a teaching session — □ □ □ □
- develop a teaching programme for clients in a chosen area of interest — □ □ □ □
- understand and use structured teaching strategies in creating a learning opportunity — □ □ □ □
- develop skills in creating learning programmes for people with limited literacy skills — □ □ □ □
- assist informal carers in developing their own teaching skills. — □ □ □ □

Session Five

I can:

- discuss the development and expression of sexuality — □ □ □ □
- evaluate the impact of learning disability on the development and expression of sexuality — □ □ □ □

	Not at all	Partly	Quite well	Very well

Session Five *continued*

- identify some common social attitudes towards the sexuality of people with a learning disability

| ☐ | ☐ | ☐ | ☐ |

- analyse the important areas of carer support with respect to sexuality in people with a learning disability

| ☐ | ☐ | ☐ | ☐ |

- discuss the legal rights of the person with learning disability, with particular reference to fertility, marriage and pregnancy.

| ☐ | ☐ | ☐ | ☐ |

Session Six

I can:

- define challenging behaviour and discuss its characteristics

| ☐ | ☐ | ☐ | ☐ |

- describe a range of possible causes of challenging behaviour in people with a learning disability

| ☐ | ☐ | ☐ | ☐ |

- consider the integrated functioning of the individual in terms of a theoretical framework of their physical, intellectual, social, emotional and spiritual dimensions

| ☐ | ☐ | ☐ | ☐ |

- discuss the social implications of challenging behaviour upon the person with a learning disability

| ☐ | ☐ | ☐ | ☐ |

- describe and discuss a behaviourist, therapeutic approach to challenging behaviour, using the behavioural analysis (ABC) chart.

| ☐ | ☐ | ☐ | ☐ |

RESOURCES SECTION

Contents

RESOURCE 1

*Charles Hannam (1975)
Parents and Mentally
Handicapped Children,
Penguin*

Mentally Handicapped Children

I was told within minutes of the birth of my first child that he had Down's syndrome. The young doctor made a genuine and honest attempt to deal with the problem; what he actually said was, 'I can tell you because you are intelligent'; it must have seemed to him that intelligence is good protection in the case of news of a disaster. But what should the poor man have said? I can't find a good formula even ten years later. I suppose that bad news is bound to be a shock even if it is broken tactfully and gently; when I was told I rushed to the library and looked for some guidance. The symptoms were all shown, but I was not reassured by pictures of hanging tongues furrowed the wrong way across, strange slit eyes, hanging bellies to indicate a lack of muscular tone, and cross-sections of brain cells. I wanted to pour out my fears and apprehensions and I wanted to know too much at the same time. The symptoms were all outlined clearly enough; what was lacking was any information of what it would be like for me and my wife. What did we have to face, and who would help us? Could we take the strain? Why had it happened, and to us? Was there possibly a cure?

I remember a kind of roar in my head, a hot, flushed feeling reminiscent of when I was a child and had done something terribly wrong. I became very active, I saw good friends, I phoned around, but I can no longer remember what any of them said, although they were all most understanding people. They tried to give me advice and comfort, but I found it hard to listen to them because I was in a state of heightened apprehension and could not cope with all the facts for some time. Even if I had been told adequately what was in store for me I still would not have found the information useful. All I knew was that there had been a disaster. Gradually I sorted things out: there was no cure, the disaster did not imply that we had done anything immoral, there was not necessarily any abnormality in us, there was no blame in the moralistic or biblical sense.

It was a great help to me to know that nothing we had done or not done could possibly have made any difference. The feeling of guilt was at first almost unbearable. I felt an almost Old Testament sense of having somehow done wrong and that this was a punishment. We had married when we were more than thirty-five years old, we had wanted to have a child, so there was no question of having made a 'mistake' and then pretending it was all intentional. It seemed to me that in that case we 'deserved' a perfect child and if it was not, there must be a reason for it. I am an ambitious person, more competitive than I care to admit, and I value my own sense of successes, however moderate they seem to outsiders. Having a mentally handicapped child made me feel that I had failed. Somehow the earliest bits of morality welled up: I should have tried harder, this was not good enough. A friend arranged that I should see a psychiatrist and I talked to him before I tried to tell my wife that the child was abnormal. At that time I must have projected some of my fears onto my wife, perhaps when I asked 'Will it drive her to breaking point?'. The psychiatrist was calm and sympathetic and I regained enough control to listen. I heard that the child would make progress, however slow it might be. The child would have a personality and would be educable in a limited sort of way.

Most important for me was that at last I could express my feelings of guilt, resentment and disappointment. Increasingly I thought that I must kill this child. This seemed to be a simple solution and all our troubles would be over. I was quite cool about this at first; I had to be alone with him and then I could do it. Before I went to see my wife that evening, I asked to see him and the sister wheeled him to me in his cot. I could see the signs of Down's syndrome clearly, the shape of his eyes, the tongue that was hanging out. I had been present at his birth – a tremendous experience – and, without knowing it then, I had diagnosed his Down's syndrome. I remember going over to him and seeing a tube in his mouth to drain away the saliva. When his nurse took the tube out, his tongue was hanging out, and I called out to my wife, 'Look, he is sticking his tongue out already'. I was terribly elated and excited at that time. We had done it, a boy, immortality had been achieved! I thought him rather ugly but then I had never seen a newly-born baby before and they are supposed to be ugly. Now I wanted to kill him and it was a very frightening thing to even think about.

Brothers and Sisters

RESOURCE 2

Charles Hannam (1975)
Parents and Mentally
Handicapped Children,
Penguin

When we had our second child who was normal, a well-meaning colleague warned me that we should have to be careful because she knew of a family where the other children had begun to behave like the abnormal child who had, therefore, been put into a home. I imagine that this piece of advice is about as valid as saying 'don't keep a dog because all your children will bark'; on the other hand, it strikes deep and adds to the apprehension and fears that abound. We have certainly watched our children very carefully, constantly looking for undue stresses and strain (and therefore probably creating them)!

Jill Ashley Miller writes in *The Times* (11 October 1971) about the time she had to decide whether to keep her child at home or not: 'The wise pediatrician had said at the time of her birth, "However hard it is, always put the normal children first".' I am sure this would be very good advice if one knew what was best for the 'normal' children and what is best for the family as a whole. For example, is it better to face up to the problem of having a mentally handicapped child together, as a family unit, or does one in a sense deny its existence by having it removed to a home?

What I have learnt is that however difficult the child is, he becomes an integral part of the family structure. To split this part off, to send him to an institution, would change the dynamics of that family's structure, and it is therefore not a step to be taken lightly. It does seem, from these interviews at least, that the position of the child in his family very much influences the kind of problems that will arise. Mrs. Mercer's Philip is the youngest of six children who accept him as their responsibility and do not like it if the parents suggest he goes into a residential unit.

Mrs. Mercer: He is the youngest of six children which I think makes it a lot easier. I have got my others who are normal; bright kids who give me the satisfaction of their intellectual achievements, and this one is really like having a friendly dog around the place. We pat him on the head and spoil him ... In fact he doesn't talk; but I suppose we don't really stimulate him enough at home, we give in to him too easily, but it has its advantages from my point of view in that I am not so wrapped up in him.

CLH: What about the rest of the family?

Mrs. Mercer Oh, they have been awfully good about it. My eldest boy, he was eleven when Philip was born, and I made my husband tell the children before I came home. I knew very well I was going to be in tears and they would ask why, so I made him tell Richard first, and Richard sat and listened to him and then he said, 'Can we keep him?' In fact they have been marvellous about him and so have their friends.

CLH: How do they treat him?

Mrs. Mercer: Indulgently. The boy who is twelve now, he got to the model-making stage at the age of six and Philip would sometimes get in the way and then of course there would be a great hoo-ha about it, but they are very fond of him, very tolerant, and very forgiving; they all look after him, too. Everybody has got their eyes and ears open for doors and things like this. The girl who is next to him in age, she is particularly fond of him. They rush into each other's arms when they have been apart for a day.

CLH: Have you sent Philip to the residential unit at the centre?

Mrs. Mercer: No. Never. The main objection comes from my children. There is a great cry of 'If he were normal you wouldn't dream of doing that'. I suggested it when we were going to my niece's twenty-first birthday party; they said they could cope and I said 'No, I think I'll put Philip into the residential unit'. 'Don't you dare', they said 'he doesn't leave until we go to school, we can wait for the bus. We are home before he comes home'. We wouldn't dare put him in for a holiday because they adore playing with him on the sands. Each year they would say 'I wonder if Philip will go in this time, shall we try that with him?' We got him in last year and couldn't get him out.

Jill Richards is the youngest of five children. She causes great difficulties to her parents, and the next brother seems to suffer because of her. In these situations it is not easy to distinguish what degree of difficulty is created by the mental handicap and what is inherent in the problems of that particular family. An older sister, Sue, seems almost unaware of her sister's peculiarities; aged sixteen, she was present at the interview.

Mrs. Richards: You know, it has caused quite a lot of problems in our family. I have a little boy, he is eight now. My husband has no time for him at all because he is all Jill now. He very seldom talks to Bill unless it's to tell him off, and Jill, like most mentally retarded children, is very affectionate, very loving, although in the next minute she can be very spiteful. My husband expects Bill to accept all this. Well you can't expect a normal healthy boy of eight to take all this and have his hair pulled. So of course he will give her one back, then my husband will have a go at him, then I have a go at my husband and that's how it goes on.

125

Simon [a seven-and-a-half-year-old brother]: My brother is mentally handicapped. It is very difficult to speak to him. I find it rather easy to understand what he is saying. I think that is because I used to sleep in the same room as him. He is nine now and it is very difficult to get him from place to place because he wants to see all the same things all the time, like rain drops: he sits on the pavement watching the drops. His favourite animals are horses, cows and sheep.

David is a very mischievous boy. His usual trick is trying to get the biscuits out of the tin on the shelf; another one is getting into my bed, he also jumps on me and fights. He likes banging on his drum and makes us all go mad. He had a guitar for his birthday and he plays that. It is very difficult for Mummy and Daddy because they don't understand him.

When we go on holiday without him I feel very sad because I miss his snoring which stops me from having bad dreams. There is only one other boy who can cope with him and that is Adam Steele. He is the son of a doctor. David is very fat because he eats lots of bread and butter and biscuits. I have known David longer and I like him a bit better than Toby (younger brother, aged four-and-a-half). We have some people who help with taking David for walks and help us. They are very nice to David.

Mrs. Hopkins: When the third child was born we had another screaming baby who kept us awake at night and I tended to reject the other two completely because I was so exhausted feeding and coping with the new baby. I think John (the eldest child, has Down's syndrome) suffered most from this because by then Richard, the second baby, was nearly three and we could explain to him what was going on, but John still was not

talking although physically he was very active ... When Jason (the third) was born John went into a residential unit and started measles while he was there. He had to go to hospital when Jason was only ten days old.

At the hospital, John would not take the food they gave him because it was not the sort of food he was used to ... I decided that the only thing to do was to spend most of the afternoon there and take food for John and myself, and so I did this; feed Jason, take him out in his carry-cot in the back of the car, park him underneath Sister's window, take John in his food, give it to him, take his nappies off and try to treat his very sore bottom, play with him and talk to him; while I was there perhaps go back and feed Jason in the car, and then come home and deal with Richard, who by then also had measles.

... I had to stop going out with three children as it was not safe to leave a pram standing with a toddler sitting on it and a baby inside it while I ran after John.

John's brother says he is miserable if the family goes on holiday without John, but at eight he is old enough to realise the problems of caring for John in a strange house, especially as he knows that John does not like the unfamiliar and would behave even more oddly than he does at home. On the other hand, the family is incomplete without him.

In the case of Mrs. Shepherd the mentally handicapped child is the younger of the two, and the older one seems 'a little bit frightened'. It may be frightening to see a brother or a sister doing things that are known to be 'naughty'.

This poses a problem for parents. Two systems of justice have to be set up which leave room for manipulation and my children often instigate mischief which David (the handicapped one) carries out very happily.

RESOURCE 3

Valerie Sinason (1992) New Approaches from the Tavistock, Free Association Books

Euphemisms and Abuse

'I've got four handicaps. I've got Down's syndrome, special needs, learning disability and mental handicap.'

Young woman with Down's syndrome.

When Nevill Symington founded what we now call the Tavistock Clinic Mental Handicap Psychotherapy and Psychology Research Workshop, he called it 'The Subnormality Workshop', using a term that was then in use. Had he founded it a few years earlier it could have been called the Mental Deficiency Workshop, the Mental Retardation Workshop or the Backwardness Workshop. Going back even further it could have been called, with no offence at the time, a Workshop on Feeblemindedness,

Imbecility, Dullards, Dotards, or Idiots.

No human group has been forced to change its name so frequently. The sick and the poor are always with us, in physical presence and in verbal terms, but not the handicapped. Euphemisms, linguistically, are words brought in to replace the verbal bedlinen when a particular word feels too raw, too near a disturbing experience (Sinason, 1984, 1986, 1989c).

Hence, although Jon Stokes and I changed the name of the Workshop to 'Mental Handicap Workshop' when we took it over in 1985 and the title expanded into 'Mental Handicap Psychotherapy and Psychology Research Workshop' when

Sheila Bichard became my co-convener in 1988, we decided it was important to try to hold onto the term 'handicap' even though the process of euphemism soon meant it was no longer a completely approved term. The Journal of Social Work Practice grappled with this in a pioneering special issue (in 1989) entitled 'Mental Handicap or Learning Difficulty?' In the USA the current favoured term is 'people with developmental disabilities', which is replacing 'mentally retarded'. This does not mean that any name in itself, whether 'handicap', 'disability', 'learning problem', or 'special needs', is necessarily better than any other. But it is important for workers to be aware that abuse lies in the relationships between people, not in the name used. As Orwell (1964) stated, 'The great enemy of language is insincerity. When there is a gap between one's real and one's declared aims, one turns as it were instinctively to long words and exhausted idioms, like a cuttlefish squirting out ink'. A young man with cerebral palsy wistfully said, 'I wish I did have a learning difficulty; not being able to learn is the least of my problems'.

Each worker introducing a new term hopes that the word brings new hope and a new period of healthy historical change. Each time a new word is coined, it is coined honourably. It is not deliberately created as a euphemism but becomes one because of the painfulness of the subject. Nearly every book on mental handicap written in the last hundred years begins with a chapter on definitions and words chosen. Each such chapter praises itself for its hopeful new term. It is therefore doing a grave disservice to past pioneers to point contemptuously to their chosen terms. Within another five years the process of euphemism will already be affecting the brave new words. On an individual level I use the terms my clients choose for themselves just as I always check how a name is pronounced and whether someone likes to be called by their formal title or their Christian name. However, individual choice is a different matter from succumbing to different pressure-group choice. It will indeed be a major step forward when internationally we all use the same term and the WHO definition is binding.

As I mentioned in the Introduction, the WHO (1980) defined impairment as any loss or abnormality of structure or function. A disability is defined as a restriction resulting from an impairment and a handicap is the disadvantage to an individual resulting from an impairment or a disability. However, a name change (as for women entering marriage) needs to think long and hard about the meaning. The term 'disability' has, in the English language, been specially linked with physical handicap for several hundred years. This means that the extension of its use for mental handicap is experienced by many as a euphemism.

The word 'euphemism' is a euphemism in itself. It derives from the Greek and literally means 'fair-speaking'. It originated in religious ceremonies where it was forbidden to speak in case the spirit would be offended by ill-omened words.

After I'm Gone What Will Happen To My Handicapped Child?

RESOURCE 4

Gerald Sanctuary (1984)
After I'm Gone What Will
Happen To My
Handicapped Child?
Condor/Souvenir Press

A Style of Life

Think of your own childhood, and the way you grew up. As the years went by you began to separate yourself from your parents and adopted a lifestyle of your own. You accepted much of what they said and did, what they wanted – most of the time – but you had to make your own way. You left school, got a job, married, found a home of your own, and began to create a life that was different.

Does your handicapped child have any right to a lifestyle of his own? Is he entitled to go his own way, to rebel, to reject your advice, to make mistakes? For many parents, the answer to these questions will be: 'Well he couldn't. He needs someone to look after him'.

So he does; but should those who care for him make every decision, do everything for him? Has he no right to make any decisions for himself? In recent years it has become ever more clear that those who suffer from handicap are 'people with a handicap', rather than 'handicapped people'. They have as much right to a life of their own as the rest of us. Decisions should not be made for them, unless there is no prospect at all of their having an opinion to express.

The title of the BBC Radio programme Does He Take Sugar? cleverly illustrates the assumption made by most people that, simply because someone has to use a wheel-chair, or is blind, he is incapable of thinking or of expressing a preference. This attitude is nonsense, and it is of course bitterly resented by those who suffer from physical handicap. There is another common assumption: that because a person is mentally handicapped he is incapable of making any sensible decision at all. It is just as insulting to a mentally handicapped woman to assume that she has no views to express about her life, as it is to ask the man pushing a wheel-chair whether its occupant takes sugar with his tea.

The point is that handicapped people are entitled to a life of their own, just like every-one else. They have preferences, and it is wrong of society to ignore these. The progress that a handicapped person makes in life, and his happiness, must depend on the chance he is given to live his own life and to make his own choices. Simply because he will sometimes make mistakes does not entitle the rest of us to remove all choice from him; we, too, have made mistakes, but we have sur-vived and are the wiser for it.

This argument cannot be taken to ridicu-lous lengths: a blind person must be dis-couraged from walking near a cliff edge; a woman in a wheelchair will require help getting up a ramp; a mentally handicapped man must be protected from entering into an expensive hire purchase contract which he cannot possibly afford. Yet this does not prevent the blind man from going out on his own, nor the woman in a wheelchair; nor should it stop a mentally handicapped per-son from entering into simple contracts, such as buying food or records, or travelling on a bus.

If we start with the assumption that there will be many things that a handicapped per-son can do and is entitled to do, and if we positively encourage him in this, we are helping to create the chance for him to develop his own style of life. His handicap must be assessed, and the right type of edu-cation, and also training, found for him. He should have the chance to enjoy leisure activ-ities, and to choose those he likes best. Throughout this book ways are suggested by which this can be achieved. If a parent has become used to doing many things for a handicapped child, it is worth considering when it might be possible for him to do some of them for himself. His Income Support Benefit is his own, not his parents'; he can be taught how to draw the money himself, and asked to give enough to his mother to buy his food. Perhaps he would like to make some of his own decisions on clothes and other things.

What does a handicapped person want? This is a better question than 'What do you think is good for him'. The answer is not sim-ple. If he is not aware that he has a choice, or has never been asked to make one, then he may happily accept the benevolent deci-sions of his parents. Matters of this kind are not confined to food or a choice of television programmes. Arthur Melsby enjoyed his walks in the park with his parents. He usu-ally travelled in a wheelchair, but he was able to get around slowly, using a stick. He was not a communicative young man and was regarded at school (which he had recently left) as very shy, if not backward. His brothers and sisters were talkative, often noisy, and because he was both handicapped and quite small he seemed almost to shrink into the background, in any group of people.

In the summer, a brass band played in the park. Arthur heard it once and was fasci-nated. They were playing at a time when he did not normally go to the park, but he demanded to go again, even offering to make his own way there, almost half-a-mile from home. It was not very convenient for his family, but arrangements were made to take him again. It was impossible to persuade him to leave until the band packed up. One of the players noticed him and stopped for a word, asking him whether he had enjoyed the performance. Arthur asked if he could hold the trumpet that the man was carrying. This was only the beginning of what was for Arthur an entirely new life: he said he wanted to learn to play a brass instrument. His family helped him and took him to and from a college of music. After a while, this took so much time that it was necessary to hire a taxi to take him there and back. His Mobility Allowance paid for part, though not all, of the cost, but one of the teachers at the college had a car and would often give him a lift home. Arthur began to play the French horn; within a year he had become reason-ably good, and after three years he joined an orchestra. His life was transformed; at home he had brass band music on the gramophone, and he practised constantly. His room had to be insulated for sound, as the rest of the family found the noise distracting, but he per-severed.

Arthur had found the life he wanted, and he never looked back. His determination might have been frustrated by a family less willing to help him branch out on his own, and less able to put up with the noise. When his brothers and sisters complained, their parents reminded them of the noise they also made, and they accepted the situation. In fact, no one felt any more that they had to 'keep Arthur occupied' or to amuse him; he was more than capable of entertaining him-self. His new-found confidence, based on having been selected for the orchestra, changed both his style of life and his spirit.

Arthur was physically but not mentally handicapped. Moira Thorogood suffered from Down's syndrome; she was short and had become plump. In the town she was well known to many people, trailing along beside her mother or father on shopping day, cheerful enough, but giving more the impression of a young child than a woman. She was 32 years old and not in fact very severely handicapped. Through a social club to which her parents belonged, arrangements were one day made for Moira to help with the catering. Her mother cooked small cakes and biscuits once a month, taking her turn with other members. Moira went with her, and on that particular day was invited to put out the cups and saucers. Her mother was very concerned in case there should be an accident, but the lady who encouraged Moira was persistent, though very friendly; she had helped at a school for physically handicapped children and assumed that Moira would like to do something useful.

After a while, Moira became an essential member of the social club, doing valuable work in and out of the kitchen. She broke no more cups or saucers than anyone else and was delighted to be able to make herself useful. Her parents, after some initial embarrassment, became very proud of what Moira could do. Later, she was asked to help in a local restaurant. She enjoyed it very much and spent most of her time working in the kitchen. She was paid a full wage and no longer needed to draw Income Support benefit. Her take-home pay was more than the benefit and she had some extra money to spend on herself. Like Arthur Melsby, Moira had found a lifestyle which suited her very well indeed.

Given different opportunities and less encouragement from the families and friends, Arthur and Moira might today be in totally different situations, he confined for the most part to his home, with few outside contacts and dependent on his family for entertainment, she going to and from a Training Centre with little prospect of meeting people and taking part in the life of the community. Neither of them, as it happens, had been given training before deciding to branch out into new activity, but both have in fact been trained – in their different ways – as a result of finding a new interest.

RESOURCE 5

Erving Goffman (1961)
Asylums: Essays on the
social situation of mental
patients and inmates,
Penguin

Asylums

A basic social arrangement in modern society is that the individual tends to sleep, play and work in different places, with different co-participants, under different authorities, and without an over-all rational plan. The central feature of total institutions can be described as a breakdown of the barriers ordinarily separating these three spheres of life. First, all aspects of life are conducted in the same place and under the same single authority. Second, each phase of the member's daily activity is carried on in the immediate company of a large batch of others, all of whom are treated alike and required to do the same thing together. Third, all phases of the day's activities are tightly scheduled, with one activity leading at a rearranged time into the next, the whole sequence of activities being imposed from above by a system of explicit formal rulings and a body of officials. Finally, the various enforced activities are brought together into a single rational plan purportedly designed to fulfil the official aims of the institution.

Individually, these features are found in places other than total institutions. For example, our large commercial, industrial and educational establishments are increasingly providing cafeterias and free-time recreation for their members; use of these extended facilities remains voluntary in many particulars, however, and special care is taken to see that the ordinary line of authority does not extend to them. Similarly, housewives or farm families may have all their major spheres of life within the same fenced-in area, but these persons are not collectively regimented and do not march through the day's activities in the immediate company of a batch of similar others.

The handling of many human needs by the bureaucratic organisation of whole blocks of people – whether or not this is a necessary or effective means of social organisation in the circumstances – is the key fact of total institutions. From this follow certain important implications.

When persons are moved in blocks, they can be supervised by personnel whose chief activity is not guidance or periodic inspection (as in many employer-employee relations) but rather surveillance – a seeing to it that everyone does what he has been clearly told is required of him, under conditions where one person's infraction is likely to stand out in relief against the visible, constantly examined compliance of the others. Which comes first, the large blocks of managed people, or the small supervisory staff, is not here at issue; the point is that each is made for the other.

In total institutions there is a basic split between a large managed group, conveniently called inmates, and a small supervisory staff. Inmates typically live in the institution and have restricted contact with

129

the world outside the walls; staff often operate on an eight-hour day and are socially integrated into the outside world.[2] Each grouping tends to conceive of the other in terms of narrow hostile stereotypes, staff often seeing inmates as bitter, secretive and untrustworthy, while inmates often see staff as condescending, high-handed and mean. Staff tend to feel superior and righteous; inmates tend, in some ways at least, to feel inferior, weak, blameworthy and guilty.[3]

Social mobility between the two strata is grossly restricted; social distance is typically great and often formally prescribed. Even talk across the boundaries may be conducted in a special tone of voice.

[2]The binary character of total institutions was pointed out to me by Gregory Bateson, and has been noted in the literature. See, for example, Lloyd E. Ohlin, Sociology and the Field of Corrections (New York: Russell Sage Foundation, 1956), pp 14, 20. In those situations where staff are also required to live in, we may expect staff to feel they are suffering special hardships and to have brought home to them a status dependency on life on the inside which they did not expect. See Jane Cassels Record, 'The Marine Radioman's Struggle for Status', American Journal of Sociology, LXII (1957), pp 351–3.
[3]For the prison version, see S. Kirson Weinberg, 'Aspects of the Prison's Social Structure', American Journal of Sociology, XLVII (1942), pp 717-26.

RESOURCE 6

Morgan, M., Calnan, N., Manning, M. (1985) The Hospital as a Social Organisation, in Morgan, M. et al. (eds) (1985) Sociological Approaches to Health and Medicine, Croom Helm, pp 152-158

Psychiatric Hospitals: Critiques and Alternatives

Sociological interest in hospitals has been particularly strong in the psychiatric field. This has been the result partly of a commitment to analyse and expose oppression in all areas of social life. In addition, psychiatric hospitals have provided a rich source of data about the limits of medical activities in practice, and the social dynamics of organisational life.

Goffman's work combined both an acute eye for detail in noticing the similar structures and processes in mental hospitals, prisons, monastic orders and so on, and an explicit moral condemnation of the impact of those total institutions on the lives of people in them.

His argument was based on the use of ideal-types. He suggested that the key process – the totality – was established by collapsing the normally separate spheres of work, home and leisure, into one monolithic social experience: a kind of 'batch living' of the kind found in factory farmed animals. The crucial phase in this process is the entry of procedures experienced by all clients going into total institutions, from army camps to prisons and hospitals (Jones, K., 1972). In essence, this amounts to the common severance of social relations on the outside and the entry into new social relations on the inside. More particularly with respect to hospitals, Goffman (1961) referred to this transition as a 'moral career'. He means by this that the changed social relationships resulting from movement into hospital include an important alteration in the patient's own identity, which becomes completely submerged by the requirements of the institution. Goffman identified three distinct aspects of this career in total institutions such as mental hospitals:

Mortification of the Self. This was achieved through the literal degrading of the person's previous status and identity, brought about the removal of their normal social props such as clothing and personal effects, the restriction of activities and movements and the requirement to engage in various demeaning practices, such as asking permission to smoke or post a letter.

Reorganisation of Self. The hospital replaces those aspects of the patient's identity it has removed: hospital clothes, hospital friends, a new status as patient, etc.

Patient Response. Goffman was well aware that his ideal-type of total institution did not always operate fully. In particular, in his discussion of the 'underlife' of asylums, he acknowledges that there are numerous means of working the system or 'making out' within the officially designated routines. Thus whereas some patients respond to the institution by colonisation, or the acceptance of their new position without enthusiasm, others become positively identified with their allotted identity in a process of conversion, while a third response is to reject the hospital's requirements, and either become withdrawn or intransigent.

The reorganised conception of the self which long-stay patients in psychiatric hospitals may come to accept has been termed 'institutionalisation' or 'institutional neurosis' which broadly corresponds with Goffman's notion of 'conversion'. Barton

(1959) gave the following definition:

Institutional neurosis is a disease characterised by apathy, lack of initiative, loss of interest most marked in things and events not immediately personal or present, submissiveness, and sometimes no expression of feelings of resentment at harsh or unfair orders. There is also a lack of interest in the future and an apparent inability to make practical plans for it, a deterioration in personal habits, toilet and standards generally, a loss of individuality and a resigned acceptance that things will go on as they are – unchangingly, inevitably and indefinitely (Barton 1959, p. 2).

References

Barton, R. (1959) *Institutional Neurosis*, Wright and Co.
Goffman, E. (1961) *Asylums*, Penguin
Jones, K. (1972) *A History of the Mental Health Services*, Routledge and Kegan Paul, London

Aetiology or Factors Associated with Institutional Neurosis

RESOURCE 7

Barton, R. (1976) *Institutional Neurosis*, John Wright & Sons. Chapter 2 'Aetiology or Factors Associated with Institutional Neurosis', pp 6-7.

The cause of institutional neurosis is uncertain. It does not seem to have a single cause. It is associated with many factors in the environment in which the patient lives. Possibly the patients react with a tendency common to most human beings to modify ambition and establish a way of life as trouble-free and secure as possible.

Though with a little ingenuity the end result might be explained in terms of conditioning, psychoanalysis, or analytical psychology, I believe the outline in general descriptive terms already given, followed by a systematic description of the factors present in the associated environment of the institution, is more valuable. As Sydenham remarked: 'In writing a natural history of diseases, every merely philosophical hypothesis should be set aside, and the manifest and natural phenomena, however minute, should be noted with the utmost exactness'. One must not confuse association with causation. It is always important to look for facts and not merely confirmation of one's hypotheses.

The idea (or construct) of the illness, institutional neurosis, has largely been obtained from reports of successful treatment by various authors. I hope that setting out these discoveries in an orderly fashion will help in recognising and treating the disorder.

The factors commonly found in the environment can be grouped conveniently under eight headings. Of course, the divisions are not absolute and these factors overlap one another.

The eight factors are:
1. Loss of contact with the outside world.
2. Enforced idleness.
3. Brutality, browbeating and teasing.
4. Bossiness of staff.
5. Loss of personal friends, possessions and personal events.
6. Drugs.
7. Ward atmosphere.
8. Loss of prospects outside the institution.

I would stress that these eight groups are clusters of factors each as different from the others as possible. They are artificial divisions of an overall picture.

Examination of these groups of factors reveals some overlap. Although experience may give the impression that correction of a single factor will in some cases bring about the dramatic recovery, i.e. discovery of a relative who begins to make regular visits, reflection makes one realise that it is difficult, if not impossible, for one factor to alter without others.

Scrutiny of each of these constituent factors separately enables us to get a better understanding of the total process of institutionalisation of which they are part.

Since writing the first edition of *Institutional Neurosis* I have reluctantly become aware that to the list of constituent factors collected some twenty years ago must be added violence, brutality, bullying, browbeating, harshness, teasing and tormenting. These loathsome practices are far more common in institutions than we realised in the 1950's. They are considered as factor number 3 in this third edition and, combined, are probably the most powerful single factor acting to subjugate patients into an apathetic, cowed, mute and timorous state. I am amazed and humiliated that with all the evidence given me by patients, relatives and

staff – especially those I was treating – I did not identify and record it years ago.

RESOURCE 8

Mr. P. Selby, School of Health Care Studies, University of Leeds

The Development of Community Care: Reports and Legislation

Produced by Mr. P. Selby, School of Healthcare Studies, University of Leeds

1801 Dr. Itard - L'Education du Sauvage d'Aveyron

1807 Dr. Itard – Confessed to partial failure

1828 Institute for Education and Training, established – Paris – followed by similar institutions in Switzerland and Germany

1837 Dr. Seguin, development of Itard's work in Paris

1846 A small school for idiots – Misses. White – 4 patients

1847 Asylum for Idiots – Park House, Highgate – under the patronage of the Duke of Cambridge and Duchess of Gloucester

1855 The institution moved to Redhill, Surrey – Earlswood Asylum

1881 561 inmates

1864 Starcross Asylum, Exeter

1868 Northern Counties Asylum,
/70 Lancaster, built and opened (all subscription hospitals) – 50-200 guineas per annum

1870s Darenth Training School – Metropolitan Asylums Board

1875 Sir Charles Trevelyan – expressed views on behalf of the Charity Organisation Society (founded 1868) – introduced the term 'feeble minded' – area for State intervention

1877 R. L. Dugdale Juke family study (American) – attempted to assess the influence of heredity on successive generations of large families of defective stock

1881 29,452 idiots in public institutions; only 3% receiving care and treatment specifically designed for them

1896 National Association for the Care of the Feeble Minded (influenced by Charity Organisation Society recommendations and M. Dendy and H. Pinsent)

1896 Cattell took up early work of Galton

1898 Lancashire and Cheshire Society for the permanent care of the feeble-minded (by Miss Dendy) – raised funds by public subscription to found the 'Mary Dendy Homes'Colony at Sandlebridge, Cheshire

1901 Galton founded the Eugenic Journal *Viometrika*

1903 Mrs. Hume Pinsent – Lancet – 'Thorough and complete scheme of State intervention' published. Work of Galton to have an influence on the eventual development of services (1889 – Hereditary Genius and Natural Inheritance)

1903 Binet – published *Etude Experimental*

1904 Galton – Eugenics laboratory set up – University College, London

1904 ROYAL COMMISSION ON THE
/8 CARE OF THE FEEBLE MINDED

1905 Binet-Simon – tests enabling 'mental age' based on norms for each age level (defined intelligence in a limited way but introduced scientific method into an area where only subjective judgement in unskilled hands might be used to give the appearance of scientific fact where no true judgement was possible)

1907 By this date some 9,000 children accommodated in special classes and special schools instituted under the Elementary Education (Defective and Epileptic Children) Act of 1899 – over half in the London area; little provision in the provinces

1907 Eugenics Education Society founded on initiative of Mrs. A. C. Grotto

1908 Galton joined society and became its president

1908 Dr. A. F. Tredgold – *Mental Deficiency*, a clinical textbook. Tredgold consulting physician to the National Association for the Care of the Feeble Minded – acted as medical expert to the Royal Commission Timing – considerable impact on the reform movement

1910 National Association for the Care of the Feeble Minded and the Eugenics

Education Society joined forces in the campaign for a Mental Deficiency Bill

1912 H. Goddard – Kallikak Family study (both Studies – Goddard & Dugdale – open to major criticism)

1912 Noted that the Home Office had received 800 resolutions from public bodies – public opinion had become formed

1912 Two private members' Bills drafted by the two Societies. Both defeated

1912 Government Bill – defeated

1913 MENTAL DEFICIENCY ACT. Idiots, imbeciles, feeble minded and moral defectives – certification and provision for segregation

1914 THE ELEMENTARY EDUCATION ACT (DEFECTIVE & EPILEPTIC CHILDREN). Special schools to provide: (i) manual training and character for the backward, but not ineducable, child; (ii) observation centre for doubtful cases, so those who were incapable of receiving education might be diagnosed and passed on to the mental deficiency authority

1914 Central Association for the Care of the Mentally Defective formed from National Association for the Feeble Minded. Secretary – Miss Evelyn Fox. By 1918 – 45 local voluntary associations.

1914 2,163 mental defectives receiving treatment in institutions built under the Idiots Act. 796 more beds end of 1914.
'Other local authorities had taken their duties seriously, and had prepared schemes for the institutional treatment of defectives. The usual policy was to acquire a fairly small building – sometimes a country house, sometimes only a workhouse – and, using this as a nucleus, to add small villas as they were required, and as building became possible again'

1915 Arthur H. Estabrook (Eugenics record office, America) follow up study on the Juke family

1921 Education Act – Sections 53-58 added to basic legislation
'The local education authority was to ascertain all defective children in the area, and had the right to enforce attendance at special schools and classes; though it was laid down as a general principle that the wishes of the parents should be consulted where possible'
Main recommendations – see pages 222 & 223, Jones (1972)

1922 Occupation Centres – first mentioned by the Board of Control. Twenty in existence, run by voluntary associations and catering for daytime train-able defectives who lived at home – restricted and supervision. Aim of centres – training low grade children and adults in good habits, self control and obedience.
Industrial Centres – training for employable defectives with a view to taking up sheltered employment

1927 THE MENTAL DEFICIENCY ACT 1927 (effects of the 1926 outbreak of encephalitis lethargic and subsequent damage to normal developing individual cannot be ignored)
– amended the definition of mental deficiency
– stressed the provision of supervision
- local authority duty to provide supervision, training and occupation

1927 5,301 beds provided by the local authorities (authorities reluctant due to costs).
'More beds were urgently needed, but the Board was beginning to realise that there were many cases which could not, in the immediate future, be treated by hospitalisation. Consequently they turned to considering methods of community care. Eventual and gradual realisation that community care was in many cases not only cheaper and more practicable, but better for the patient (despite the continued influence of the segregation of mental defectives being the best form of management)'

1929 Report of the Wood Committee

1929 Local Government Act – dismantled the Poor Law framework. Transfer of certain Poor Law institutions to the mental deficiency authorities and responsibility of mental defectives receiving out-relief. Growth of community services/care noted to be considerable (following the 1929 Report). By 1934, 59,004 receiving some form of community care. Nine hostels in operation, and occupation and industrial centres rise to 191

1934 Brock Committee Report
– concluded that sterilisation should be legalised - on a voluntary basis, and subject to stringent safeguards
– Government unwilling to introduce such a controversial measure.
'While the practical and ethical objections have not lost force, belief in the hopelessness of the condition of the submerged tenth had been modified by social work practice in the intervening years'

1938 (O.H.E.) 60 local authorities run, and 95 voluntary facilities of this type, offering 4,000 places

1944 EDUCATION ACT (Malin 1980).

Continued to define a class of children as incapable of receiving education at school – excluded from universal education system set up by the Government

1945 America. Study Kingsley and Hyde. Studies 600 people rejected by the military for reasons of mental deficiency (Malin). They found a majority were both socially and economically self supporting

1946 NATIONAL HEALTH SERVICE ACT. Control of certified institutions passed from the local councils to the Minister of Health – colonies became hospital (legacy of accumulated wisdom on the care and segregation of the mentally handicapped)

1948 Formation of the National Health Service (and associated problems – low priority regarding policy – M.H. services – administrative structure – medicalisation of mental handicap)

1951 Hartzler – found 73% of girls discharged from a state institution were wholly or partially successful in adjustment to life in the community

1953 America. Charles follow-up study to Ballers (1936) group of person adjudged mentally deficient (Malin). Traced 151 of original 206 – 80%

married with less children per family than national average; 83% self supporting. (Early prognoses for these people had been unduly pessimistic)

1954 England. O'Connor & Tizzard – survey a 2% sample of patients in twelve mental deficiency institutions. 50% of sample were reported as not requiring special nursing or supervisory care – followed earlier criticisms of existing training methods in hospitals as being irrelevant to outside employment – seriously under-estimating the potential of the trainees for working in the community

1954 Hilliard supports above conclusion with 'more concrete evidence'

1954/7 Royal Commission on Mental Illness and Mental Deficiency leading to the 1959 Mental Health Act

1959 MENTAL HEALTH ACT – emphasis on voluntary rather than compulsory admission, and shift from hospital to community provisions emphasised (for a concise account, see Malin et al., 1980, pp 50-51)

Reference

Malin, N. (1980), Services for the Mentally Handicapped in Britain, Croom Helm, London

RESOURCE 9

John O'Brien for the Georgia Advocacy Office, Atlanta.

Adapted for CMH by Alan Tyne of the Community and Mental Handicap Educational and Research Association.

Vicious and Virtuous Circles

Vicious Circles

The most extreme example of devaluation for a person is what sociologists call a 'deviancy career'. The way a person is seen as different becomes synonymous with the person's identity. In a way, the person's handicap becomes his/her occupation – it dominates every aspect of their life.

The deviancy career is a vicious circle in which a person meets widely held stereotypes and comes to embody them. Here is an example of how the vicious circle works:

- a child has an impairment in ability which is labelled 'severe mental handicap'
- he and his family meet a service system which they will come to depend upon for help. The service system is designed around the belief that people who are labelled 'severely handicapped' are, by nature, incompetent
- the service system advises the family that their son will always 'need' hospital care, which it offers
- although the hospital tries hard, it simply doesn't have the resources to give the

support and training he needs. Worse, staff believe he will 'probably never develop very much', so he becomes with each passing year less and less capable than others of the same age
- the person's continuing incompetence justifies continued pessimism about his ability which leads to continued deprivation of learning opportunities.

The most vicious circles are the ones that begin with what 'everybody knows'. As far as people with handicaps are concerned, assumption about their growth potential, about their right to enjoy opportunities, or about the capacity of others to accept and respond positively to them and their needs.

One of the strangest parts of the vicious circle is its effect on what people see. For instance, ' everybody knows that young children who are severely handicapped can't join the same playgroups and nurseries as other children do'. When you show people who 'know' that this is exactly what is beginning to happen, logic says that what 'everybody knows' should change. But vicious circles aren't logical. What usually happens is that those who 'know' say, 'Those children must have been mislabelled; they aren't really severely handicapped at all', or 'Well, the severely handicapped children I know must be a lot more severely handicapped than these children are'. Progress only begins when someone questions what 'everybody knows' and turns it from a prediction that defines the future into an undesirable situation to be changed – the change from 'It's a shame nothing can be done', to 'Letís see what we can do to change this ...'

The vicious circle has two bad effects. First, many people with handicaps 'live down' to low expectations and reduced opportunities. Second, negative stereotypes of people with handicaps are strengthened as people observe the way some official 'helpers' treat them and see the negative result of opportunity deprivation on their lives. The two negative results work together to strengthen each other. Everybody loses. People with handicaps are blocked from potential growth – a person's label becomes a life sentence. And society and its services fail to learn more effective ways to support and teach. Left to itself, the vicious circle becomes more and more powerful as it feeds on itself.

There is an important use for vicious circles. If we can understand them, we can work systematically to reverse their effects. Ignoring the vicious circle focuses attention to its most obvious part, the handicapped person's assumed deficits. This over-attention leaves only one target for the change – the person – and few ways to accomplish it. With few effective tools for change, we are likely to become pre-occupied with describing what is the matter with people at the expense of working to change it. This breeds hopelessness.

Attending to the whole vicious circle gives us more targets and more tools for change. We can work to change expectations: our own in the short run; the larger society's in the long run. We can work to expand the opportunities available for handicapped people. And, in the context of expanding expectations and opportunities, we can work to change the person who is handicapped.

Consider this example of reversing a vicious circle (described in Gold, 1976[1]). Marc Gold, a University of Illinois researcher, designed a training programme to teach 22 long-term institution residents, 15 of whom were labelled severely or profoundly mentally retarded (IQ scores for the group ranged from 17–52), and all of whom were blind, or deaf and blind, to perform complex industrial assembly tasks. All 22 people learned to perform the task effectively (in terms of accuracy) and moderately efficiently (in terms of rate of production per hour).

The success of this training effort rests on four assumptions which were sufficient to reverse the vicious circle.

The researchers selected a task that challenged what 'everybody knows' about severely handicapped people's vocational ability. Rather than a trivial task, they chose a task that would require special training for any worker regardless of intelligence (positive beliefs about people with handicaps).

Everyone was seen as a learner. The teachers expected that all 22 learners would successfully perform the task if they were given adequately powerful instruction (well defined, expanded expectations).

No one was excluded from training and each learner had as much opportunity to learn as was necessary (increased opportunity).[2]

The project staff recognised that the possibility of people's learning depends on the teacher's ability to design instructions and modify teaching strategies when they did not work. Gold states this in two principles:
– the more difficult it is for a person to acquire a task, the more a teacher must know about the task; and
– the more the designer of training knows about the task, the less the learner needs to know at the beginning.

The consumer is always right; if a person is not learning, the teacher must change his/her approach. Under these conditions, people with handicaps teach their teachers how to teach more effectively (powerful teaching).

But the changes did not stop there – the work situation. In a film interview[3], the staff described other ways the vicious circle was being reversed. They noted that the training programme demonstrated that people trained did not 'live down' to living unit staff's expectations. Despite initial scepticism, everyone learned. Once this became clear, it was no longer possible for staff to hold the same low expectations. They began to raise their expectations and expand opportunities for learning in other areas. A 'virtuous circle' – in which everybody wins – has been initiated.

1 M. W. Gold, Task Analysis: A statement and an example using acquisitions and production of a complex assembly task by the retarded blind, Exceptional Children, 1976, No. 43, pp 78–84

2 In fact, the learner who mastered the task most rapidly took 9 trials; the learner who required the most teaching to master the task took 196 trials. Interestingly, no significant connection was found between people's IQ and their ability to learn this task.

3 The film is called Try Another Way. It was made in Indianapolis, Indiana, in 1976. You can hire it from Concord Films Council, 201 Felixstowe Road, Ipswich, Suffolk. Tel: 01473 76012.

RESOURCE 10

Macclesfield Health Authority, (1991) EQUAL – IF, Evaluating Quality Using Assessment of Lifestyles – Individuals First, pp ii-iv, Mersey Regional Health Authority

Overview of the Content of the Eight Dimensions of Lifestyle Covered in EQUAL – IF

Domesticity

This section addresses the user's experience as a 'domestic person' in the home. The questions focus around two areas of rights:

● practical access, i.e. facilities, equipment and the presence of support to enable the user to become involved in domestic life to the limit of her or his ability and desire;

● development of competence, i.e. is the user given the opportunity to learn and develop domestic skills at an organisational, practical and decision-making level.

Physical well-being

Questions relating to the user's 'health' in the fullest sense of the word, are addressed. The sub-sections deal with well-being at a primary, secondary and tertiary level. Within these areas, the adequacy of the practical, medical, educational, legal and psychological support being offered to the user is considered.

Empowerment

The issues of how the user is 'empowered' is a theme which runs through the instrument. This section, however, looks at aspects of the user's lifestyle where there are clear and quantifiable ways of considering the extent to which she or he is empowered as a citizen with full rights and responsibilities.

Pattern of daily life

Perhaps self-explanatory, this section deals with daily rhythms and routines. It attempts to assess whether the user is being enabled to live in a way which not only meets her or his personal needs but corresponds to mainstream, valued patterns of timing of activities.

Social well-being

Not surprisingly, this section of questions is particularly value-laden. Issues of social integration, freedom of choice and rights are intertwined in a section which attempts to assess how fully the user is enabled to fulfil her or his desires and needs, both as a social being and a member of the community.

Occupation/vocation

In this section, the ways in which the user is supported to fulfil her or his wishes and rights for access to meaningful 'occupation' are addressed. Rather than evaluating the quality of the occupation itself, questions focus around the ways in which the user is made aware of occupational options and then introduced and supported in the chosen option.

Environment

This section deals with the physical environment of the user's living accommodation. The questions can be seen to focus around four areas of rights:

● practical access, i.e. do the design and content of the accommodation fulfil basic requirements which allow the user to make full use of her or his home: this includes the assessment of practical aids and adaptations which would minimise the impact of the user's particular disability on her or his quality of life in the home;

● comfort-value imagery, i.e. does the accommodation project a positive image of its occupant(s) (included are considerations of age/culture-appropriateness, distantiating features, etc.);

● development of competence, i.e. does the home offer an environment where the user has the opportunity to learn and develop competencies around the 'hazards of every-day-life', without being exposed to unnecessary or unacceptable areas of risk.

Organisation of the service

The final section of the instrument deals with aspects of the service – its organisation, management, and delivery – which have a direct or an indirect effect on how the user might experience attainments of their rights.

REFERENCES

ABEL, E. L. and SOKOL, R. J. (1987) 'The incidence of foetal alcohol syndrome and the economic impact of foetal alcohol syndrome and related anomalies', in *Drug and Alcohol Dependence* 19: (1987) 51–70.

ATKINSON, D. and WILLIAMS, F. (eds) (1990) *Know Me As I Am: An anthology of prose, poetry and art by people with learning difficulties*, Hodder and Stoughton.

BANK-MIKKELSEN, N. (1980) 'Denmark', in Flynn, R. J. and Nirsch, K. E. (eds) (1980) Normalisation, Social Integration and Community Services, Austin, Texas, Pro-Ed.

BANNISTER, A. (1992) 'Recognising abuse', in Stainton, R. et al. (eds) (1992) Child Abuse and Neglect: Facing the Challenge, B. T. Batsford Ltd.

BARNES, C. (1994) *Disabling Imagery and the Media*, Ryburn/British Council of Organisations of Disabled People.

BARNES, C. (1994) 'Images of disability', in French, S. (1994) On Equal Terms: Working with disabled people, Butterworth Heinemann.

BARTON, R. (1976) *Institutional Neurosis* (3rd Edition), J. Wright.

BECK, C. M., RAWLINS, R. P. and WILLIAMS, S. R. (1988) *Mental Health Psychiatric Nursing: A holistic life cycle approach* (2nd ed.), C V Mosby, St. Louis.

BROWN, H. SMITH, H. (1992) *Normalisation: a reader for the nineties*, Tavistock/Routledge.

BROWN, H., and SMITH, H. (1992) *'Assertion, not Assimilation: A feminist perspective on the normalisation principle*', in Brown, H. and Smith, H. (eds.) (1992) Normalisation: A reader for the nineties, Tavistock/Routledge.

BURNS, J. (1993) *'Sexuality, sexual problems and people with a learning disability*', in Ussher, J. M. and Baker, C. D. (eds.) (1993) Psychological Perspectives on Sexual Problems: New directions in theory and practice, Routledge.

CHRISTIE, R. et al. (1982) 'Lesch-Nyhan Disease: Clinical experience with nineteen patients', cited in: Murphy, G. and Wilson, B. (eds.) (1982) Self Injurious Behaviour, BIMH Publications.

CRAFT, A. (1987) *Mental Handicap and Sexuality Issues and Perspectives*, Costello.

CUMMING, M. and GOLDSTONE, L. (1991) EQUAL – IF *Evaluating Quality Using Assessment of Lifestyles – Individuals First*, Mersey Regional Health Authority and Macclesfield Health Authority.

DERBYSHIRE COALITION OF DISABLED PEOPLE (1993) Info 10, DCDP, Claycross, Derbyshire.

DERBYSHIRE, P. and WHITAKER, S. (1990) 'The Final Challenge', *Nursing Times*, Jan. 10, Vol. 86, No 2.

DIXON, H. (1988) *Sexuality and Mental Handicap*: An educator's resource book, Learning Development Aids.

DOAK, C.C., DOAK, L.G. and ROOT, J. H. (1996) *Teaching Patients with Low Literacy Skills*, J B Lippincott, Philadelphia.

EDGERTON, R. (1976) *Deviance: A cross cultural perspective*, Benjamin/Cummings.

ELLIS, W. G., McCULLOCH, J. R. and CARLEY, C. L. (1974) 'Pre-senile dementia in Down's syndrome', *Neurology*, February 1974 Vol 24. No. 2.

EMERSON, E. (1992) *'What is Normalisation?'*, in Brown, H., Smith, H, (eds.) (1992) Normalisation: A reader for the nineties, Tavistock/Routledge.

EMERSON, E. et al. (1987) Developing Services for People with Severe Learning Difficulties and Challenging Behaviours, cited in Mansell, J. (1994) 'Challenging Behaviour. The prospect for change: A keynote review', *British Journal of Learning Disabilities*, Vol. 22, 1, 2-5.

FINKELSTEIN, V. (1993) 'From caring or curing to defining disabled people', in Walmsley, J. et al. (1993) Health Welfare and Practice: *Reflecting on roles and relationships*, Sage Publications/Open University Press.

FLEMMING, I., KROESE, B. S. (eds.) (1993) *People with Learning Disabilities and Severe Challenging Behaviour*, Manchester University Press.

FOUCAULT, M. (1965) *Madness and Civilisation: A history of insanity in the age of reason*, Tavistock.

FRENCH, P. (1983) *Social Skills for Nursing Practice*, Chapman and Hall.

FRENCH, S. (1994) *On Equal Terms: Working with disabled people*, Butterworth Heinemann.

GOFFMAN, E. (1961) *Asylums: Essays on the social situation of mental patients and inmates*, Penguin.

HANNAM, C. (1975) *Parents and Mentally Handicapped Children*, Penguin.

HARRIS, P. (1993) 'The nature and extent of aggressive behaviour amongst people with learning disability (mental handicap) in a single health district', *Journal of Intellectual Disability Research*, No. 37.

HORWOOD, W. (1987) *Skallagrigg*, Penguin.

HMSO (1959) *Mental Health Act* 1959, HMSO.

HMSO (1990) *National Health Service and Community Care Act* 1990, HMSO.

JONES, K. (1972) *A History of the Mental Health Services*, Routledge and Kegan Paul

JONES, K. L. and SMITH, D. W. (1973) 'Recognition of foetal alcohol syndrome in early infancy', *The Lancet*, Nov 3, 1973, pp 999-1002.

KING'S FUND (1980) *An Ordinary Life: Comprehensive locally-based residential services for mentally handicapped people*, King's Fund.

LION, E. (ed.) (1982) *Human Sexuality in Nursing Process*, John Wiley & Sons, New York.

LITTLE, B .B., SNELL, L. M., ROSENFELD, C. R., GILSTROPE, L. C. and GANT, N. F. (1990) 'Failure to recognise foetal alcohol syndrome in newborn infants', *American Journal of Diseases in Children*, Oct 90 Vol. 144 No. 10.

LOWE, F. et al. (1993) 'Verbal self-regulation', cited in Flemming, I., Kroese, B. S. (eds.) (1993) *People with Learning Disability and Severe Challenging Behaviour*, Manchester University Press.

MACKINTOSH, N. (1984) *In search of a new theory of conditioning*, in Ferry, G. (ed.) (1984) *The Understanding of Animals*, Blackwell and New Scientist.

MAGER, R. F. (1972) *Goal Analysis*, C A Fearon, Belmont.

MANSELL, J. (1994) 'Challenging behaviour: the prospect for change: a keynote review', *British Journal of Learning Disabilities*, Vol. 22.

MARKHAM, G. (1986) 'Epilepsy', *Nursing 8*, Nursing Times Series.

MASLOW, A. H. (1968) *Towards a Psychology of Being*, Van Nostrand, New York.

McBRIAN, J. and FELCE, D. (1992) *Working with People who have Severe Challenging Behaviour*, British Institute of Learning Disabilities.

MacNAMARA, M. (1995) *Lifeskills: A positive approach*, Souvenir Press.

MORGAN, M., CALNAN, N. and MANNING, M. (1985) 'The hospital as a social organisation', in Morgan, M. et al. (eds.) (1985) Sociological Approaches to Health and Medicine, Croom Helm.

MORRIS, J. (1993) *Independent Lives?: Community care and disabled people*, Houndmills/Macmillan.

NIRJE, B. (1969) *The Normalization Principle and its Human Management Implications* in Kugel, R. B. and Wolfensberger, W. (eds.) (1969) Changing Patterns in Residential Services for the Mentally Retarded, Presidential Committee on Mental Retardation, Washington D.C.

O'BRIEN, J. (1987) *'A guide to life style planning: using the activities catalogue to integrate services and natural support systems'*, in Wilcox, B.W. and Bellamy, G.T. (eds) The Activities Catalogue: An alternative curriculum for youth and adults with severe disabilities, Brookes, Baltimore.

O'BRIEN, J. and TYNE, A. (1981) *The Principle of Normalisation: A foundation for effective services*, Campaign for Mentally Handicapped People.

OLIVER, M. (1990) *The Politics of Disablement*, Macmillan.

OSWIN, M. (1971) *The Empty Hours*, Penguin.

OWENS, G. and BIRCHENALL, P. (1979) *Mental Handicap: The social dimensions*, Pitman Medical.

PROSSER, G. (1989) 'Down's syndrome, Alzheimer's disease and reality orientation, *Mental Handicap*, Vol. 17, June, B.I.M.H. Publication.

REED, W. B. and HEAD, A. (1993) cited in Flemming I. and Kroese, B. S. (1993) *People with Learning Disability and Severe Challenging Behaviour*, Manchester University Press.

RICHARDSON, S. (1971) 'Handicap, appearance and stigma', *Social Science and Medicine 5*, 621-628.

RYAN, J. and THOMAS, F. (1980) *The Politics of Mental Handicap*, Penguin.

SANCTUARY, G. (1984) *After I'm Gone What Will Happen to My Handicapped Child?*, Condor/Souvenir Press.

SCULL, A. (1979) *Museums of Madness*, Penguin.

SHANLEY, E. and STARRS, T. A. (1993) *Learning Disabilities: A handbook of care*, 2nd edn., Churchill Livingstone.

SINASON, V. (1992) *Mental Handicap And The Human Condition: New approaches from the Tavistock*, Free Association Books.

THOMPSON, S. B. (1994) 'A neuropsychological test battery for identifying dementia in people with Down's syndrome', *British Journal of Developmental Disabilities*, July, Vol. 40: 2: 79, pp 135–142.

TOMLINSON, S. (1982) *A Sociology of Special Education*, Routledge and Kegan Paul.

TURNBULL, C. (1980) *The Mountain People*, Picador.

UNITED NATIONS (1971) *Declaration on the Rights of Mentally Retarded Persons*, United Nations, Geneva.

WALMSLEY, J. (1994) *Learning Disability: Overcoming the barriers?* in French, S. (1994) On Equal Terms: Working with disabled people, Butterworth Heinemann.

WESTCOTT, H. (1994) *Abuse of Children and Adults with Disabilities*, NSPCC.

WHITTAKER, A., GARDNER, S. and KERSHAW, J. (1991) *Service Evaluation by People with Learning Difficulties*, King's Fund Centre.

WOLFENSBERGER, W. (1972) *Normalization: the principle of normalization in human services.* National Institute of Mental Retardation, Toronto.

WOLFENSBERGER, W. (1983) 'Social Role Valorization: A proposed new term for the principal of normalization', *Mental Retardation* 21: 234–9.

WOLFENSBERGER, W. and THOMAS, S. (1983) PASSING: *Program Analysis of Service Systems Implementation of Normalization Goals*, National Institute on Mental Retardation, Toronto.

GLOSSARY

Acquired handicap –

A handicap sustained as a consequence of trauma, usually in adulthood.

Backward chaining –

A process of error-free learning that begins at the end point of the learning chain and builds up each part of the task in small stages, until the total learning is achieved.

Community care –

The provision of care within local communities, usually in 'ordinary' housing, such as small residential homes, or within the family.

Conditioning –

A type of learning where response results from a neutral stimulus which previously had been repeatedly presented in conjunction with the stimulus that originally elicited the response.

Condition visibility –

A disability or disfigurement that is noticeable to the casual observer.

Conservatism corollary –

Wolfensberger's theory that the greater the visible difference from the 'norm' a person appears to be, the greater is the need for that individual to present to society a 'conformist' or 'conservative' appearance.

Dual diagnosis –

The presence of two diagnosed conditions usually referring to the combined diagnosis of learning disability and mental health problems.

Eugenics –

A movement relating to the development and improvement of offspring.

Forward chaining –

A process of error-free learning that commences at the starting point of the learning chain and builds up each part of the task in small stages, until the total learning is achieved.

Functional analysis –

An approach which aims to discover the pre-disposing factors to challenging behaviour and to understand how the inappropriate behaviour serves the individual.

Institutionalisation –

The debilitating impact of life in a total institution, leading to loss of self-identity and personal power.

Institutional neurosis –

The presence of clearly designated negative changes in appearance and behaviour that are the consequence of living in large wards in hospitals. A phase coined by *Barton, R.* (1976).

Life chance –

The opportunities that are present in an individual's life.

Life cycle –
The chronological progress through life, beginning at birth and ending with old age and eventual death.

Micro-institutionalisation –
The impact of a lifestyle within a small residential home in the community that is similar to the consequences of the very negative environment evident in the large hospital.

Mixed economy of care –
The delivery of care involving the public, private and voluntary sectors that crosses the boundaries of health and social services.

Normalisation –
The philosophy of care that underpins the movement towards 'an ordinary life' for people with learning disabilities. Key author Wolfensberger.

Prompting –
Something which strengthens a learned response.

Reinforcement –
Rewarding behaviour – making it more likely to happen again.

Self-stimulatory hypothesis –
A theory which suggests that every person needs a certain level of stimulation. People with a learning disability may be under-stimulated because of the nature of their environment.

Social Darwinism –
The extrapolation of Darwin's theory of natural selection into social theories to justify the 'survival of the fittest' (or, more exactly, the extinction of the unfit) in human society.

Social role valorisation –
The creation of valued social roles for people with a learning disability. Key author Wolfensberger.

Stigma –
A negative value attributed to a mental, emotional or physical condition.

Task analysis –
The breaking down into stages of learning that assists in creating the process of error-free learning.

Total institution –
A place of residence and work where a large number of individuals, cut off from wider society, together lead an enclosed, formally administered life.

Vicious circle –
A series of life events that start from a negative assumption about the potential of an individual and lead towards the degradation of ability: a self-fulfilling prophecy.

Virtuous circle –
The antithesis of a vicious circle, in that a skill or positive attribute of an individual is highlighted, so leading to further positive life experiences.